POCKET GUIDE TO THE NATIONAL ELECTRICAL CODE®

1987 EDITION

MARVIN J. FISCHER, P.E.

PRENTICE-HALL, INC.
Englewood Cliffs, NJ 07632

Library of Congress Cataloging-in-Publication Data

Fischer, Marvin J. (date)
Pocket guide to the National Electrical Code, 1987 edition.

Includes index.
1. Electric engineering—Insurance requirements—Handbooks, manuals, etc. I. National Fire Protection Association. National Electrical Code. II. Title.
TK260.F47 1987 621.319'24'0218 87–14421
ISBN 0–13–684606–8

Editorial/production supervision: Karen S. Fortgang
Interior design: Mary Carnis
Manufacturing buyer: Margaret Rizzi

Printed in the United States of America

10 9 8 7 6 5 4 3 2 1

ISBN 0-13-684606-8 025

Prentice-Hall International, Inc., *London*
Prentice-Hall of Australia Pty. Limited, *Sydney*
Prentice-Hall Canada Inc., *Toronto*
Prentice-Hall Hispanoamericana, S.A., *Mexico*
Prentice-Hall of India Private Limited, *New Delhi*
Prentice-Hall of Japan, Inc., *Tokyo*
Prentice-Hall of Southeast Asia Pte. Ltd., *Singapore*
Editora Prentice-Hall do Brasil, Ltda., *Rio de Janeiro*

CONTENTS

List of Tables ix

Preface xiii

1 General 1

100 Definitions 2
110 Requirements for Electrical Installations 2

2 Wiring Design and Protection 5

200 Use and Identification of Grounded Conductors 5
210 Branch Circuits 7
215 Feeders 18
220 Branch-Circuit and Feeder Calculations 20
225 Outside Branch Circuits and Feeders 33

230 Services 37
240 Overcurrent Protection 47
250 Grounding 53
280 Surge Arresters 71

3 Wiring Methods and Materials 72

300 Wiring Methods 72
305 Temporary Wiring 79
310 Conductors for General Wiring 79
318 Cable Trays 83
320 Open Wiring on Insulators 112
321 Messenger-Supported Wire 113
324 Concealed Knob-and-Tube Wiring 114
325 Integrated Gas Spacer Cable—Type IGS 115
326 Medium Voltage Cable—Type MV 115
328 Flat Conductor Cable—Type FCC 116
330 Mineral-Insulated, Metal-Sheathed Cable—Type MI 118
331 Electrical Nonmetallic Tubing 120
333 Armored Cable—Type AC 120
334 Metal-Clad Cable 122
336 Nonmetallic-Sheathed Cable—Types NM and NMC 124
337 Shielded Nonmetallic-Sheathed Cable—Type SNM 126
338 Service-Entrance Cable—Types SE and USE 127
339 Underground Feeder and Branch-Circuit Cable—Type UF 128
340 Power and Control Tray Cable—Type TC 129
342 Nonmetallic Extensions 130
344 Underplaster Extensions 130
345 Intermediate Metal Conduit 131
346 Rigid Metal Conduit 134
347 Rigid Nonmetallic Conduit 137
348 Electrical Metallic Tubing 139
349 Flexible Metallic Tubing 141

350 Flexible Metal Conduit 142
351 Liquidtight Flexible Metal Conduit and Liquidtight Flexible Nonmetallic Conduit 144
352 Surface Metal Raceways and Surface Nonmetallic Raceways 146
353 Multioutlet Assembly 147
354 Underfloor Raceways 148
356 Cellular Metal Floor Raceways 148
358 Cellular Concrete Floor Raceways 149
362 Wireways 149
363 Flat Cable Assemblies—Type FC 149
364 Busways 149
365 Cablebus 149
366 Electrical Floor Assemblies 149
370 Outlet, Device, Pull and Junction Boxes, Conduit Bodies and Fittings 150
373 Cabinets and Cutout Boxes 156
374 Auxiliary Gutters 157
380 Switches 158
384 Switchboards and Panelboards 159

4 Equipment for General Use 164

400 Flexible Cords and Cables 164
402 Fixture Wires 167
410 Lighting Fixtures, Lampholders, Lamps, Receptacles, and Rosettes 168
422 Appliances 176
424 Fixed Electric Space Heating Equipment 181
426 Fixed Outdoor Electric De-icing and Snow-Melting Equipment 189
427 Fixed Electric Heating Equipment for Pipelines and Vessels 192
430 Motors, Motor Circuits, and Controllers 194
440 Air Conditioning and Refrigerating Equipment 209

445 Generators 214
450 Transformers and Transformer Vaults 214
460 Capacitors 214
470 Resistors and Reactors 214
480 Storage Batteries 214

5 Special Occupancies 215

500 Hazardous (Classified) Locations 215
501 Class I Locations 217
502 Class II Locations 224
503 Class III Locations 230
510 Hazardous (Classified) Locations, Specific 232
511 Commercial Garages, Repair and Storage 233
513 Aircraft Hangars 233
514 Gasoline Dispensing and Service Stations 233
515 Bulk Storage Plants 233
516 Spray Application, Dipping and Coating Processes 233
517 Health Care Facilities 233
518 Places of Assembly 233
520 Theaters and Similar Locations 233
530 Motion Picture and Television Studios and Similar Locations 233
540 Motion Picture Projectors 233
545 Manufactured Building 233
547 Agricultural Buildings 233
550 Mobile Homes and Mobile Home Parks 233
551 Recreational Vehicles and Recreational Vehicle Parks 233
553 Floating Buildings 233
555 Marinas and Boatyards 233

6 Special Equipment 234

600 Electric Signs and Outline Lighting 234

604 Manufactured Wiring Systems 234
605 Office Furnishings 234
610 Cranes and Hoists 234
620 Elevators, Dumbwaiters, Escalators, and Moving Walks 234
630 Electric Welders 234
640 Sound-Recording and Similar Equipment 234
645 Electronic Computer/Data Processing Systems 234
650 Organs 234
660 X-Ray Equipment 234
665 Induction and Dielectric Heating Equipment 234
668 Electrolytic Cells 234
669 Electroplating 234
670 Industrial Machinery 234
675 Electrically Driven or Controlled Irrigation Machines 234
680 Swimming Pools, Fountains, and Similar Installations 234
685 Integrated Electrical Systems 234
690 Solar Photovoltaic Systems 235

7 Special Conditions **235**

700 Emergency Systems 235
701 Legally Required Standby Systems 235
702 Optional Standby Systems 235
705 Interconnected Electric Power Production Sources 235
710 Over 600 Volts, Nominal—General 235
720 Circuits and Equipment Operating at Less Than 50 Volts 235
725 Class 1, Class 2, and Class 3 Remote-Control, Signaling, and Power-Limited Circuits 235
760 Fire Protective Signaling Systems 235
770 Optical Fiber Cables 235
780 Closed-Loop and Programmed Power Distribution 235

8 Communications Systems 235

800 Communication Circuits 235
810 Radio and Television Equipment 235
820 Community Antenna Television and Radio Distribution Systems 235

9 Tables and Examples 236

Tables 237
Examples 264

LIST OF TABLES

TABLE NO.	TITLE
210-21(b)(2)	Maximum Cord- and Plug-Connected Load to Receptacles 12
210-21(b)(3)	Receptacle Ratings for Various Size Circuits 13
210-24	Summary of Branch-Circuit Requirements 16
220-3(b)	General Lighting Loads by Occupancies 20
220-11	Lighting Load Feeder Demand Factors 24
220-13	Demand Factors for Nondwelling Receptacle Loads 25
220-18	Demand Factors for Household Electric Clothes Dryers 26
220-19	Demand Loads for Household Electric Ranges, Wall-Mounted Ovens, Counter-Mounted Cooking Units, and Other Household Cooking Appliances over 1¾ kW Rating 28

TABLE NO.	TITLE
220-20	Feeder Demand Factors for Kitchen Equipment—Other Than Dwelling Unit(s) 30
220-30	Optional Calculation for Dwelling Unit Load in kVA 30
220-32	Optional Calculation—Demand Factors for Three or More Multifamily Dwelling Units 31
220-34	Optional Method—Demand Factors for Feeders and Service-Entrance Conductors for Schools 33
250-94	Grounding Electrode Conductor for AC Systems 68
250-95	Minimum Size Equipment Grounding Conductors for Grounding Raceway and Equipment 69
310-16	Ampacities of Not More Than Three Single Insulated Conductors, Rated 0 through 2000 Volts, in Raceway in Free Air and Ampacities of Cable Types AC, NM, NMC, and SE Based on Ambient Air Temperature of 30°C (86°F) 84
310-17	Ampacities of Single Insulated Conductors, Rated 0 through 2000 Volts, in Free Air Based on Ambient Air Temperature of 30°C (86°F) 88
310-18	Ampacities of Three Single Insulated Conductors Rated 0 through 2000 Volts, 110° to 250°C, in Raceway in Free Air Based on Ambient Air Temperature of 40°C (104°F) 92
310-19	Ampacities for Single Insulated Conductors Rated 0 through 2000 Volts, 110° to 260°C, in Free Air Based on Ambient Air Temperature of 40°C (104°F) 96
310-22	Ampacities of Three Insulated Conductors, Rated 0 through 2000 Volts, Within an Overall Covering (Three Conductor Cable), in Raceway in Free Air Based on Ambient Air Temperature of 30°C (86°F) 100
310-23	Ampacities of Two or Three Single Insu-

TABLE NO.	TITLE
	lated Conductors, Rated 0 through 2000 Volts, Supported on a Messenger, Based on Ambient Air Temperature of 40°C (104°F) 104
310-24	Ampacities for Bare or Covered Conductors Based on 40°C Ambient, 80°C Total Conductor Temperature, 2 Feet (610 mm) per Second Wind Velocity 108
346-10	Radius of Conduit Bends (Inches) 132
346-10	Exception: Radius of Conduit Bends (Inches) 133
370-6(a)	Metal Boxes 156
370-6(b)	Volume Required per Conductor 154

CHAPTER 9

TABLE NO.	TITLE
1	Percent of Cross Section of Conduit and Tubing for Conductors 237
2	Maximum Number of Fixture Wires in Trade Sizes of Conduit or Tubing 238
3A	Maximum Number of Conductors in Trade Sizes of Conduit or Tubing 240
3B	Maximum Number of Conductors in Trade Sizes of Conduit or Tubing 242
3C	Maximum Number of Conductors in Trade Sizes of Conduit or Tubing 244
4	Dimensions and Percent Area of Conduit and of Tubing 246
5	Dimensions of Rubber-Covered and Thermoplastic-Covered Conductors 248
5A	Aluminum Building Wire/Nominal Dimensions and Areas 252
6	Dimensions of Lead-Covered Conductors: Types RL and RHL 254
7	Dimensions of Asbestos-Varnished-Cambric Insulated Conductors: Types AVA, AVB, and AVL 256
8	Conductor Properties 258
9	AC Resistance and Reactance for 600 V Cables, 3 Phase, 60 Hz, 75°C 262

PREFACE

The *Pocket Guide to the National Electrical Code®* is intended for use as a convenient reference guide for architects, engineers, electrical designers, electrical contractors, electricians, manufacturers, inspectors, teachers, students, and all those who use the code in their work. The reader should have a basic knowledge of electricity and the *National Electrical Code®* * or be using this book together with other instructional material in the study of electricity, electrical design, and construction. This book is not intended to replace the *National Electrical Code®* but rather be used with it. It is intended to provide the user with a reference book of those topics in the *NEC®* * which occur most frequently to the user in a form that can be carried at all times where it might prove inconvenient to carry a copy of the complete *National Electrical Code®*.

The *NEC®* is probably the most referenced and widely distributed single electrical code in use today. It is adapted into law in most jurisdictions in the United States: town, village, city, county, and state. Most federal and state agencies adapt this code in whole or in part or refer to specific pertinent sections and paragraphs. Naturally, there are some exceptions. It is safe to say that if your work or profession in any way touches the electrical field, a thorough knowledge of the *National Electrical Code®* may be quite important, if not an absolute necessity.

Let us examine for a moment who might be using the *NEC®* and for what purpose. The reader will note that it is not uncommon today to find one person falling into more than one category. Those people in the design profession—architects, engineers, and electrical designers—must surely refer to the Code in their everyday work. Not only must the design conform to the Code theoretically, but practically the work must be capable of being installed in conformance with the Code so as to provide a safe installation. It should be noted that the *National Electrical Code®* is not and should not be used as a design specification. This is noted in paragraph 90–1(c) of the Code and will be discussed later. It should be used as a guide for a minimum provision of an essentially safe installation. Adequate space must be provided, and proper wire size and insulation must be used for specific purposes. These are just a few of the many topics of concern for design professionals. All are aimed at providing safe installation.

Once a project is designed, it must be built. This is accomplished primarily by electrical contractors, their licensed electricians, and helpers. The *National Electrical Code®* includes provisions for the proper installation and construction of electrical work. How to pull wire through conduit, number of wires in a conduit, color coding to be used, and where, how, and under what circumstances the various types of wire and cable may be used are just an example of the many areas of concern.

The supplies and equipment used in an electrical installation must meet minimum requirements that are enumerated in the Code. They must also meet a minimum set of standards, such as color coding and markings on wire and cable, thickness and gauge of materials, and voltage ratings. Hence the manufacturers are constantly referring to the *NEC*® to ensure that their products meet the minimum standards set forth and therefore are salable.

When work is finished, before being used, it must be inspected by the enforcing authority of the Code. It is at this point that many differences in interpretation emerge. Naturally, it would be nice if we could all come up with one meaning or intent for a given set of rules. Unfortunately, this is not always the case. The inspector must be as familiar with the Code as any other person using it and in some cases more so. He may become the final arbiter before a judge's decision.

Finally, let us not forget those who will take our place, the students and their teachers. The *National Electrical Code*® becomes a useful instructional tool and therefore must be understood and used by the instructor and learned by the student.

It has been found that people using it need to refer to certain topics in the *National Electrical Code*® more frequently than other topics. Some are of concern on a daily basis, whereas others may appear infrequently and then only when a special project is in progress. A copy of the complete *National Electrical Code*® is a necessity and should always be available to the reader. However, a book containing a discussion of only those paragraphs that occur most frequently, and one that is more convenient to carry than the entire Code, will obviously be an excellent aid for daily use. To add to the ease of use of this handy reference, it should be of a size that could easily be carried in a pocket and not take up space in a case. This *Pocket Guide to the National Electrical Code®* was developed and written to fill that need and provide that convenience.

The topics and parts of the *NEC®* chosen for this book are those that the author felt would be most useful to the reader on a daily basis. Less frequently used parts of the *NEC®* are noted by Article headings for reference purposes only. The manner in which the material is presented is not intended to appear as official interpretations by the author. It represents the author's opinions developed over many years in the electrical field and through activity on NFPA committees. Official or formal interpretations may be obtained only from the NFPA and through a definite procedure outlined in the Code. It is also recommended that the authorities having jurisdiction be consulted. This book refers to the 1987 edition of the *National Electrical Code®*.

I would like to dedicate this book to my wife, *Ruth*, and children, *Michael*, *Cheryl*, *Cathi*, and *Wendy*, and grandson, *Brian*, for their encouragement and patience during its writing.

Marvin J. Fischer

1

GENERAL

Chapter 1 consists of two articles (100 and 110). Before discussing this chapter a few comments are necessary concerning Article 90, Introduction, which precedes Chapter 1. Article 90 covers the purpose of the Code, the scope and arrangement of the Code, enforcement, the method of obtaining formal interpretations, examination of equipment for safety, wiring planning, and metric units. Section 90-1, Purpose, indicates that the *National Electrical Code®* is *not* intended to be used as a design specification. It contains only provisions for safety. Compliance with the Code does not ensure that the installation is adequate for good service, or that it is convenient or efficient. These criteria are left to other qualified persons, such as electrical designers or engineers.

ARTICLE 100
DEFINITIONS

This article contains definitions. Other definitions may be found in sections for specific installations, such as Section 517-2 (Health Care Facilities) and Section 550-2 (Mobile Homes and Mobile Home Parks).

ARTICLE 110
REQUIREMENTS FOR ELECTRICAL INSTALLATIONS

A. General

110-1 Mandatory Rules and Explanatory Material

110-2 Approval

110-3 Examination, Identification, Installation and Use of Equipment

110-4 Voltages

110-5 Conductors

110-6 Conductor Sizes

110-7 Insulation Integrity

110-8 Wiring Methods

110-9 Interrupting Rating

110-10 Circuit Impedance and Other Characteristics

The entire electrical circuit, including all devices and wire, must be capable of clearing a fault before extensive damage takes place.

110-11 Deteriorating Agents

110-12 Mechanical Execution of Work

110-13 Mounting and Cooling of Equipment

110-14 Electrical Connections

110-16 Working Space about Electrical Equipment (600 Volts, Nominal or Less)

(a) Clearances for three types of installation are noted. Type 1 consists of live exposed parts on one side and no live or grounded parts on the other side of the working space or guarded live parts (insulating material used) on both sides of the working space. Type 2 consists of exposed live parts on one side and grounded parts on the other side. Type 3 consists of exposed live parts on both sides. For voltages to ground between 0 and 150 V, a minimum clear distance of 3 ft is required in all cases. For voltages to ground between 151 and 600 V, Type 1 requires 3 ft clearance, Type 2 requires 3½ ft, and Type 3 requires 4 ft. No working space is required behind assemblies where no renewable parts are on the back and all wiring is accessible from the front (such as panelboards). A minimum of 30 in. is required in front of electrical equipment as well as a 90° opening.

(f) Headroom of 6¼ ft is required above service equipment, motor control centers, panelboards, or switchboards, with the exception of dwelling units not in excess of 200 A.

110-17 Guarding Live Parts (600 Volts, Nominal or Less)

110-18 Arcing Parts

110-19 Light and Power from Railway Conductors

110-21 Marking

110-22 Identification of Disconnecting Means

B. Over 600 Volts, Nominal

110-30 General

110-31 Enclosure for Electrical Installations

110-32 Workspace about Equipment

110-33 Entrance and Access to Workspace

110-34 Workspace and Guarding

2

WIRING DESIGN AND PROTECTION

ARTICLE 200
USE AND IDENTIFICATION OF GROUNDED CONDUCTORS

A. General Provisions

200-1 Scope

Article 200 covers the identification of terminals, grounded conductors in premises wiring systems, and identification of grounded conductors.

200-2 General

The wiring systems of all premises must have a grounded conductor that is identified as stated in Section 200-6. Exceptions to this are noted in Sections 210-10, 215-7, 250-3, 250-5, 250-7, 503-13, 517-104, 668-11, 668-21, and 690-14 Exception. When the grounded conductor is insulated, the insulation must be usable on ungrounded conductors in the same circuits where the voltage is less than 1 kV. For solidly grounded neutral systems of 1 kV or more [Section 250-152(a)], the insulation rating must be 600 V or more.

200-3 Connection to Grounded Systems

Premises Wiring. When the premises wiring system has a grounded conductor, it must be connected to a supply system which also has a grounded conductor.

200-6 Means of Identifying Grounded Conductors

(a) A white or gray covering or insulation is required on insulated grounded conductors of size No. 6 or smaller. MI cable must have distinctive marking at the terminations.

(b) When the insulated grounded conductor is larger than No. 6, it can be identified the same as conductors smaller than No. 6 or have white markings at its terminations. Requirements for multiconductor flat cable No. 4 or larger are noted.

In both cases (a) and (b), distinctive white markings at the conductor terminations may be used instead of the white or gray coverings if qualified persons perform the maintenance. Exceptions are noted.

(c) When the grounded conductor is in a flexible cord, it must have a gray or white cover or be identified in accordance with Section 400-22.

(d) Requirements for grounded conductors of different systems.

200-7 Use of White or Natural Gray Color

White or gray continuous coverings on a conductor or white or gray markings on terminations can be used only to identify the grounded conductor. These colors may be used for undergrounded conductors: (1) where they are recolored at each termination to show the intended use, (2) for three- and four-way switch loops to supply the switch and recolored at termination, (3) for ungrounded conductors in flexible cords, and (4) in circuits of less than 50 V when permitted by Section 250-5(a).

200-9 Means of Identification of Terminals

200-10 Identification of Terminals

When conductors are to be attached to more than "one side" of a circuit, they must have the device terminals identified. This is not necessary when the connection is evident, in lighting and appliance branch-circuit panelboards, in single-pole devices which are connected to only one side of the line, and in devices rated over 30 A—other than polarized attachment plugs and receptacles. Polarized attachment plugs and receptacles must have the terminal for the grounded conductor marked white. The terminal for the equipment grounding conductor must be marked in green. The terminal for the grounded conductor in screw-shell devices is the one connected to the screw shell. If there is a lead connected to the screw shell, it must be white or gray.

200-11 Polarity of Connections

ARTICLE 210
BRANCH CIRCUITS

210-1 Scope

Article 210 applies to all branch circuits except motor loads. When a branch circuit supplies this type of load in combination with a motor load, both this article and Article 430 must be followed. When the branch circuit supplies only motor loads, Article 430 must be followed.

210-2 Other Articles for Specific-Purpose Branch Circuits

The rules for branch circuits in the following table amend or supplement this article as noted.

	Article	Section
Air-Conditioning and Refrigerating Equipment		440-5
		440-31
		440-32
Busways		364-9
Class 1, Class 2, and Class 3 Remote-Control, Signaling, and Power-Limited Circuits	725	
Closed-Loop and Programmed Power Distribution Systems	778	
Cranes and Hoists		610-42
Electronic Computer/Data Processing Systems		645-2
Electric Signs and Outline Lighting		600-6
Electric Welders	630	
Elevators, Dumbwaiters, Escalators, and Moving Walks		620-61
Fire Protective Signaling Systems	760	
Fixed Electric Space Heating Equipment		424-3
Fixed Outdoor Electric De-icing and Snow-Melting Equipment		426-4
Induction and Dielectric Heating Equipment	665	

Infrared Lamp Industrial Heating Equipment		422-15
		424-3
Marinas and Boatyards		555-4
Mobile Homes and Mobile Home Parks	550	
Motion Picture and Television Studios and Similar Locations	530	
Motors and Motor Controllers	430	
Organs		650-6
Recreational Vehicles and Recreational Vehicle Parks	551	
Sound-Recording and Similar Equipment		640-6
Switchboards and Panelboards		384-22
Systems Over 600 Volts, Nominal	710	
Systems Under 50 Volts	720	
Theaters and Similar Locations		520-41
		520-52
		520-62
X-Ray Equipment		660-2
		517-143

210-3 Classifications

Branch circuits are classified according to the maximum permitted rating or setting of their overcurrent device. Generally, they are classified as 15, 20, 30, 40, and 50 A.

210-4 Multiwire Branch Circuits

Multiwire branch circuits are permitted. They can only supply line to neutral load, except if it supplies one piece of equipment or if all ungrounded conductors of the circuit are opened by the overcurrent device simultaneously.

210-5 Color Code for Branch Circuits

In general, the grounded conductor must have a continuous white or gray cover. When different systems are installed in the same enclosure, one grounded conductor must have a white covering. The other system grounded conductors must have a white cover with a stripe of another color, except green. MI cables are marked at the terminals. When only qualified persons perform maintenance and supervision of the installations, distinctive white markings may be used at the terminals in lieu of the white or gray coverings.

210-6 Branch-Circuit Voltage Limitations

(a) The voltage between conductors cannot be greater than 120 V for lighting fixtures and cord- and plug-connected loads of less than 1380 V-A in dwelling units, hotel and motel guest rooms, and the like.

(b) Circuits not exceeding 120 V to ground can supply auxiliary equipment of electric discharge lamps, utilization equipment, and medium-base shell lampholders or other types within their voltage rating.

(c) Circuits between 120 and 277 V to ground can supply mogul-base screw-shell lampholders within their voltage rating, auxiliary equipment to electric discharge lamps, and utilization equipment.

(d) 600 V between conductors.

210-7 Receptacles and Cord Connectors

In general, 15- and 20-A branch circuits are to have grounding receptacles installed. Exceptions are listed where no means of grounding exists.

210-8 Ground-Fault Protection for Personnel

(a) Dwelling Units. All 125-V single-phase 15- and 20-A receptacles installed in bathrooms, garages, within 6 ft of kitchen sinks, in boathouses, and outdoors with access to the dwelling on grade must have ground-fault circuit interrupter protection. This is not required in a garage if the receptacles are not readily accessible or for an appliance occupying a specific area connected with a cord and plug. A minimum of one must also be installed in a basement.

(b) Hotels and Motels. Ground-fault circuit interrupters are required in bathrooms of guest rooms on all 125-V single-phase 15- and 20-A outlets.

210-9 Circuits Derived from Autotransformers

210-10 Ungrounded Conductors Tapped from Grounded Systems

B. Branch-Circuit Ratings

210-19 Conductors—Minimum Ampacity and Size

(a) General. Generally, conductors must have a capacity not less than the maximum load. Conductors for multioutlet branch circuits for receptacles must be rated at least as that of the branch circuit. Various tables are supplied. If the conductors are sized so that the maximum voltage drop on the branch circuit to the outlet is not greater than 3% and the total voltage drop for both feeder and branch circuit is not greater than 5%, a reasonable efficiency of operation will be provided.

(b) Household Ranges and Cooking Appliances. Ratings cannot be less than the rating of the load. In cases of ranges of 8¾ kW or more, the minimum circuit rating is 40 A. Neutrals and conductors are permitted to be smaller in accordance with the Code.

(c) Other Loads. Ratings must be sufficient for the loads supplied, but in no case can a conductor be smaller than No. 14. Exceptions are made for tap conductors and fixture wires and cords.

210-20 Overcurrent Protection

The equipment and conductors used on branch circuits must be protected by overcurrent devices. The ratings or settings are set forth in Section 240-3 for conductors, Section 200-2 for equipment, and Section 210-21 for outlet devices. An exception is made for tap conductors, fixture wire, and cords which are permitted in Sections 210-19(c) and 240-4. These are protected by the branch-circuit protection.

210-21 Outlet Devices

(a) Lampholders connected to a branch circuit rated at more than 20 A must be a heavy-duty type.

TABLE 210-21(b)(2) Maximum Cord- and Plug-Connected Load to Receptacle

Circuit Rating Amperes	*Receptacle Rating Amperes*	*Maximum Load Amperes*
15 or 20	15	12
20	20	16
30	30	24

TABLE 210-21(b)(3) Receptacle Ratings for Various Size Circuits

Circuit Rating Amperes	*Receptacle Rating Amperes*
15	Not over 15
20	15 or 20
30	30
40	40 or 50
50	50

(b) Receptacles. A single receptacle can have a rating only equal to or larger than the rating of the individual branch circuit it is on. The maximum load from a cord and plug connection is shown in Table 210-21(b)(2). The ratings of receptacles where there is more than one on a circuit are shown in Table 210-21(b)(3). If the branch circuit rating is more than 50 A, then the receptacle rating must be at least as large as the branch circuit.

210-22 Maximum Loads

The total load cannot exceed the rating of the branch circuit. Article 430 governs only motor-operated loads on a circuit. Article 440 governs only air conditioning and refrigeration equipment on a circuit. If the circuit combines motor-operated loads that are fastened in place and larger than ⅛ hp, the total load is 125% of the largest motor plus the sum of all other loads. When the circuit contains inductive lighting loads supplied by ballasts or transformers, the actual ampere ratings should be used. Continuous loads must be not more than 80% of the branch-circuit rating. The 80% rating is not applied for motor loads having demand factors, circuits that have been derated as a result of more than three conductors in a raceway, and assemblies that are listed for 100% rating continuous operation.

210-23 Permissible Loads

(a) 15- and 20-A branch circuits can supply lighting loads, utilization equipment, or a combination. The rating of one cord- and plug-connected utilization equipment cannot be more than 80% of the branch-circuit ratings. Connected utilization equipment cannot be more than 50% of the branch-circuit rating where both connected and cord-and-plug loads are used.

(b) 30-A branch circuits can supply heavy-duty lampholders in fixed lighting units in all occupancies except dwelling units. They can also supply utilization equipment in all occupancies. One cord- and plug-connected utilization equipment cannot be more than 80% of the branch circuit rating.

(c) 40- and 50-A branch circuits supply the same lighting loads as the 30-A branch circuit, connected cooking appliances in any occupancy, and infrared heating units in occupancies except dwelling units. They can supply fastened in place cooking appliances in dwelling units.

(d) If the branch circuit is larger than 50 A, it can only supply nonlighting loads.

210-24 Branch-Circuit Requirements—Summary

Table 210-24 provides a summary of branch-circuit requirements other than those required in Section 220-3(b). A dwelling unit branch circuit can only serve one dwelling unit, with one exception.

C. Required Outlets

210-50 General

A cord connection is considered a receptacle outlet if it is supported by a permanently installed cord pendant. When it is known that a flexible cord will be used, a receptacle outlet should be installed. Appliance outlets are to be installed within 6 ft of the location of the appliance.

210-52 Dwelling Unit Receptacle Outlets

(a) General Provisions. Receptacle outlets must be installed in dwelling units so that a receptacle outlet is not more than 6 ft from any point in a wall space along the floor line. This applies to wall spaces 2 ft wide or larger, those containing sliding panels (exterior walls only), and those containing fixed room dividers. A wall space is an unbroken wall along the floor (unbroken by doors, fireplaces, etc.) Each wall space 2 ft wide or more is considered separately. However, more than one wall, if connected, is considered one wall space, such as around a corner. Receptacles are to be spaced equally. Receptacles in floors and in lighting fixtures or appliances 5½ ft above the floor are not counted. The areas that this applies to are kitchen, family room, dining room, living room, parlor, library, den, sunroom, bedroom, recreation room, and similar types of rooms.

(b) Countertops. A receptacle is to be installed in each countertop space wider than 12 in. in kitchens and dining rooms. If an installed appliance blocks a receptacle, the receptacle is not counted.

(c) Bathroom. A minimum of one wall receptacle is to be installed next to the basin.

(d) Outdoor Outlets. A minimum of one outdoor outlet is to be installed for one-family houses. A two-family house must have at least one outdoor outlet for each unit. The outlets are to be at grade level.

(e) Laundry Areas. A minimum of one outlet is to be installed in the laundry area. This is not required in multifamily dwelling units where laundry rooms are provided or laundry facilities are not individually installed.

(f) Basements and Garages. A minimum of one receptacle is to be installed in the basement and garage of a one-family dwelling. Refer to Sections 210-8(a)(2) and (a)(4).

TABLE 210-24 Summary of Branch-Circuit Requirements

(Type FEP, FEPB, SA, TW, RH, RHW, RHH, THHN, THW, THWN, and XHHW conductors in raceway or cable)

Circuit Rating	*15 Amp*	*20 Amp*	*30 Amp*	*40 Amp*	*50 Amp*
Conductors (min. size)					
Circuit wires*	14	12	10	8	6
Taps	14	14	14	12	12
Fixture wires and cords			Refer to Section 240-4		

Overcurrent Protection	*15 Amp*	*20 Amp*	*30 Amp*	*40 Amp*	*50 Amp*
Outlet devices					
Lampholders permitted	Any type	Any type	Heavy duty	Heavy duty	Heavy duty
Receptacle rating†	15 Max. Amp	15 or 20 Amp	30 Amp	40 or 50 Amp	50 Amp
Maximum Load	*15 Amp*	*20 Amp*	*30 Amp*	*40 Amp*	*50 Amp*
Permissible load	Refer to Section 210-23(a)	Refer to Section 210-23(a)	Refer to Section 210-23(b)	Refer to Section 210-23(c)	Refer to Section 210-23(c)

* These gages are for copper conductors.

† For receptacle rating of cord-connected electric-discharge lighting fixtures, see Section 410-30(c).

210-60 Guest Rooms

Guest rooms in a hotel or motel must comply with Section 210-52 unless otherwise required for permanently installed furniture. Refer to Section 210-8(b).

210-62 Show Windows

A minimum of one receptacle is required for each 12 linear feet or major fraction of a show window. It is to be measured at the maximum width and the receptacle to be installed above the window.

210-63 Rooftop Heating, Air-Conditioning, and Refrigeration Equipment Outlet

210-70 Lighting Outlets Required

(a) Dwelling Units. Every habitable room, as well as outdoor entrances and exits, attached garages, hallways, stairways, and bathrooms, must have a minimum of one lighting outlet controlled by a wall switch. A receptacle is acceptable in place of the lighting outlet in habitable rooms. Remote automatic or central control can be used in hallways, outdoor entrances, and stairways. When an attic, utility room, underfloor space, or basement is used for storage or equipment requiring service, it must have a minimum of one lighting outlet.

(b) Guest Rooms. Guest rooms in hotels, motels, and similar installations must have a minimum of one lighting outlet or receptacle connected to a wall switch.

ARTICLE 215
FEEDERS

215-1 Scope

215-2 Minimum Rating and Size

If a three-wire feeder supplies more than two two-wire branch circuits or two or more three-wire branch circuits, it must be sized for at least 30 A. The same is true of a two-wire feeder supplying two or more two-wire branch circuits. If a feeder carries the total load of the service entrance conductors and the ampacity of the service entrance conductor is 55 A or less, the feeder must be sized at least the same.

215-3 Overcurrent Protection

Refer to Article 240, Part A.

215-4 Feeders with a Common Neutral

215-5 Diagram of Feeders

215-6 Feeder Conductor Grounding Means

If equipment grounding conductors are required, refer to Section 250-57.

215-7 Ungrounded Conductors Tapped from Grounded Systems

Permitted with a switching device with a pole in each ungrounded conductor.

215-8 Means of Identifying Conductor with Higher Voltage to Ground

215-9 Ground-Fault Protection

When a feeder supplies 15- and 20-A receptacle branch circuits, the branch-circuit ground-fault circuit interrupter may be installed in the feeder instead of the requirements of Section 210-8 and Article 305.

ARTICLE 220
BRANCH-CIRCUIT AND FEEDER CALCULATIONS

A. General

220-1 Scope

220-2 Voltages

220-3 Computation of Branch Circuits

(a) Continuous and Noncontinuous Loads. The rating of the branch circuit is to be at least that of the noncontinuous load plus 125% of the continuous load.

(b) Lighting Load for Listed Occupancies. Table 220-3(b) lists the minimum load required based on floor area, which is calculated using outside dimensions. Where an area cannot be used (such as a garage or open porch), it does not have to be included. It should be noted that these values are a minimum and may not provide for an adequate installation.

TABLE 220-3(b) General Lighting Loads by Occupancies

Type of Occupancy	*Unit Load per Sq. Ft. (Volt-Amperes)*
Armories and auditoriums	1
Banks	3½*
Barber shops and beauty parlors	3
Churches	1
Clubs	2
Court rooms	2
Dwelling units†	3
Garages—commercial (storage)	½
Hospitals	2
Hotels and motels, including apartment houses without	

TABLE 220-3(b) (continued)

Type of Occupancy	*Unit Load per Sq. Ft. (Volt-Amperes)*
provisions for cooking by tenants†	2
Industrial commercial (loft) buildings	2
Lodge rooms	1½
Office buildings	3½*
Restaurants	2
Schools	3
Stores	3
Warehouses (storage)	¼
In any of the above occupancies except one-family dwellings and individual dwelling units of two family and multi-family dwelling units of:	
Assembly halls and auditoriums	1
Halls, corridors, closets, stairways	½
Storage spaces	¼

For SI units: one square foot = 0.093 square meter.

† All general use receptacle outlets of 20-ampere or less rating in one-family, two-family and multifamily dwellings and in guest rooms of hotels and motels [except those connected to the receptacle circuits specified in Section 220-4(b) and (c)] shall be considered as outlets for general illumination, and no additional load calculations shall be required for such outlets.

* In addition a unit load of 1 volt-ampere per square foot shall be included for general purpose receptacle outlets when the actual number of general purpose receptacle outlets is unknown.

(c) Other Loads: All Occupancies. In occupancies not listed in Table 220-3(b), all receptacle outlets must be rated at a minimum of 180 V/A.

Outlets for heavy-duty lampholders are to be rated at 600 V/A. Outlets for specific loads must be the rating of the load. Motor loads are covered in Sections 430-22 and 430-24 and in Article 440.

Multioutlet assemblies need only be counted as one outlet (1½ A) for each 5-ft length or, where many appliances are likely to be connected, each 1-ft length. Table 220-19 can be used for loads for household electric ranges. Show-window lighting can be calculated as 200 VA per foot. Outlets for frames and switchboards in telephone exchanges are not covered by this section. Demand factors in Section 220-18 can be used for household electric dryers.

(d) Loads for Additions to Existing Installations. Loads for additions to dwelling units greater than 500 square feet are to be calculated in accordance with Section 220-3(b). Additions to circuits should be calculated as noted in Section 220-3(b) and (c). Loads for other than dwelling units are to be calculated as noted in Section 220-3(b) and (c).

220-4 Branch Circuits Required

(a) Number of Branch Circuits. The number of branch circuits is to be calculated from the total load and should be capable of supplying the lighting and appliances.

(b) Small-Appliance Branch Circuits—Dwelling Unit. At least two 20-A appliance branch circuits are to be installed for the appliance load in the kitchen, pantry, breakfast room, and dining room. They are to have no other outlets on them. The electric clock need not be connected to an appliance circuit. Counter top receptacles in a kitchen must be supplied by at least two appliance branch circuits. These circuits can supply required outlets in other rooms. Switched receptacles are permitted under special conditions.

(c) Laundry Branch Circuits—Dwelling Unit. At least one 20-A branch circuit with no other outlets on it must be installed for laundry receptacles.

(d) Load Evenly Proportioned among Branch Circuits. The load calculated using Table 220-3(b) is to be divided as evenly as possible among all branch circuits.

B. Feeders

220-10 General

(a) Ampacity and Computed Loads. Feeders must be able to supply the required load. They must be sized to supply the connected load with applied allowable demand factors.

(b) Continuous and Noncontinuous Loads. For a continuous load or combination of continuous and noncontinuous loads, the rating of the feeder overcurrent device and ampacity of the ungrounded service conductor must be at least 125% of the continuous load plus the noncontinuous load. The 125% factor can be reduced to 100% where the article is rated for continuous operation.

220-11 General Lighting

To calculate the general lighting load, use the demand factors in Table 220-11.

220-12 Show-Window Lighting

Use at least 200 VA per linear foot.

220-13 Receptacle Loads—Nondwelling Units

Receptacle loads may either be lumped in with lighting loads and demand factors from Table 220-11 or figured separately and demand factors from Table 220-13 used. The load is to be figured at not more than 180 V/A per receptacle.

220-14 Motors

Calculate as directed by Sections 430-24, 430-25, and 430-26.

TABLE 220-11 Lighting Load Feeder Demand Factors

Type of Occupancy	*Portion of Lighting Load to Which Demand Factor Applies (Volt-Amperes)*	*Demand Factor Percent*
Dwelling units	First 3000 or less at	100
	From 3001 to 120,000 at	35
	Remainder over 120,000 at	25
Hospitals*	First 50,000 or less at	40
	Remainder over 50,000 at	20
Hotels and motels—including apartment houses without provision for cooking by tenants*	First 20,000 or less at	50
	From 20,001 to 100,000 at	40
	Remainder over 100,000 at	30
Warehouses (storage)	First 12,500 or less at	100
	Remainder over 12,500 at	50
All others	Total volt-amperes	100

* The demand factors of this table shall not apply to the computed load of feeders to areas in hospitals, hotels, and motels where the entire lighting is likely to be used at one time, as in operating rooms, ballrooms, or dining rooms.

TABLE 220-13 Demand Factors for Nondwelling Receptacle Loads

Portion of Receptacle Load to Which Demand Factor Applies (volt-amperes)	*Demand Factor Percent*
First 10 kVA or less	100
Remainder over 10 kVA at	50

220-15 Fixed Electric Space Heating

Generally, the load is to be calculated at 100% of the connected load. If, however, the total load is less as a result of intermittent operation or diversity, the authorities can reduce the calculated load. Optional calculations as shown in Sections 220-30 and 220-31 can be used in a dwelling unit and as shown in Section 220-32 for multifamily units. The feeder load current rating can never be less than that of the largest branch circuit it supplies.

220-16 Small Appliance and Laundry Loads—Dwelling Units

Use 1500 volt-amperes for each small appliance and laundry branch circuit called for in Section 220-4(b) and (c). This can be included in the general lighting load, and demand factors of Table 220-11 applied.

220-17 Appliance Load—Dwelling Units

A demand factor of 75% can be applied to nameplate ratings of four or more appliances in a dwelling. This does not apply to electric ranges, clothes dryers, and space heating or air-conditioning equipment.

220-18 Electric Clothes Dryers—Dwelling Units

Use a load of 5000 VA or the nameplate rating, whichever is larger. Demand factors listed in Table 220-18 can be used.

TABLE 220-18 Demand Factors for Household Electric Clothes Dryers

Number of Dryers	*Demand Factor Percent*
1	100
2	100
3	100
4	100
5	80
6	70
7	65
8	60
9	55
10	50
11-13	45
14-19	40
20-24	35
25-29	32.5
30-34	30
35-39	27.5
40 and over	25

220-19 Electric Ranges and Other Cooking Appliances—Dwelling Units

This section applies to household electric ranges, wall-mounted ovens, counter-mounted cooking units, and other household cooking units larger than $1\frac{3}{4}$ kW. For those units the demand load in Table 220-19 can be used. kVA and kW are considered equivalent for this section.

For single-phase ranges on a three-phase four-wire feeder, use twice the number of units between two phases. Reference to the code should be made for five notes to this table concerning ranges between 12 and 27 kW and between 1¾ and 8¾ kW for alternate allowable means of calculation.

220-20 Kitchen Equipment—Other Than Dwelling Units

This section applies to commercial cooking equipment, dishwasher booster heaters, water heaters, and other kitchen equipment. Demand factors shown in Table 220-20 can be used. They apply to thermostatic controlled or intermittently used kitchen equipment, not air conditioning, space heating or ventilating equipment. The feeder must always be larger than the sum of the two largest kitchen equipment loads.

220-21 Noncoincident Loads

If two loads on the same feeder will not be operating simultaneously, the smaller of the two can be omitted for calculation purposes.

220-22 Feeder Neutral Load

The feeder neutral load is by definition the maximum unbalanced load between the neutral and one ungrounded conductor. In five-wire two-phase systems the load is then multiplied by 140%. A factor of 70% is used in the case of household electric ranges, wall-mounted ovens, and counter-mounted cooking units. A factor of 70% may also be used for load more than 200 A in systems with three-wire dc or single-phase ac; three-phase, four-wire; and two-phase, five-wire. Reduction of neutral capacity in a four-wire wye-connected three-phase system is not permitted for loads of data processing, electric discharge lighting, and the like.

TABLE 220-19 Demand Loads for Household Electric Ranges, Wall-Mounted Ovens, Counter-Mounted Cooking Units, and Other Household Cooking Appliances over 1¾ kW Rating

	*Maximum Demand (See Notes)**	*Demand Factors Percent (See Note 3)**	
Number of Appliances	*Column A (Not over 12 kW Rating)*	*Column B (Less Than 3½ kW Rating)*	*Column C (3½ kW to 8¾ kW Rating)*
1	8 kW	80	80
2	11 kW	75	65
3	14 kW	70	55
4	17 kW	66	50
5	20 kW	62	45
6	21 kW	59	43
7	22 kW	56	40
8	23 kW	53	36
9	24 kW	51	35
10	25 kW	49	34
11	26 kW	47	32
12	27 kW	45	32

13	28 kW	43	32
14	29 kW	41	32
15	30 kW	40	32
16	31 kW	39	28
17	32 kW	38	28
18	33 kW	37	28
19	34 kW	36	28
20	35 kW	35	28
21	36 kW	34	26
22	37 kW	33	26
23	38 kW	32	26
24	39 kW	31	26
25	40 kW	30	26
26-30	15 kW plus 1 kW for each range	30	24
31-40		30	22
41-50	25 kW plus ¾ kW for each range	30	20
51-60		30	18
61 and over		30	16

Column A to be used in all cases except as otherwise permitted in Note 3.

* Refer to the NEC for notes.

TABLE 220-20 Feeder Demand Factors for Kitchen Equipment—Other Than Dwelling Unit(s)

Number of Units of Equipment	*Demand Factors Percent*
1	100
2	100
3	90
4	80
5	70
6 and over	65

C. Optional Calculations for Computing Feeder and Service Loads

220-30 Optional Calculation—Dwelling Unit

Table 220-30 can be used as an optional method for calculating loads in a dwelling unit with a mini-

TABLE 220-30 Optional Calculation for Dwelling Unit Load in kVA

Largest of the Following Four Selections:

(1) 100 percent of the nameplate rating(s) of the air conditioning and cooling, including heat pump compressors.

(2) 65 percent of the nameplate rating(s) of the central electric space heating including integral supplemental heating in heat pumps.

(3) 65 percent of the nameplate rating(s) of electric space heating if less than four separately controlled units.

(4) 40 percent of the nameplate rating(s) of electric space heating of four or more separately controlled units.

Plus: 100 percent of the first 10 kVA of all other load. 40 percent of the remainder of all other load.

mum load of 100 A and a single service of three-wire 120/240 V and 120/208Y V. Other loads in the table include 1500 volt-amperes for small appliance and laundry circuits, 3 volt-amperes per square foot for general lighting, and nameplate ratings of fastened in place appliances, wall-mounted ovens, motors, low-power-factor loads, and counter-top cooking units.

220-31 Optional Calculations for Additional Loads in Existing Dwellings

This section applies only to existing 120/240-V and 120/208Y-V three-wire services. It gives an alternate means of calculating loads. Refer to the section in the Code.

220-32 Optional Calculation—Multifamily Dwelling

This section permits an alternate means of calculation of feeder and service loads when each dwelling is supplied by a maximum of one feeder, has electric cooking, and has electric space heating or air conditioning. The alternate calculation is based on the demand factors shown in Table 220-32. These demand factors apply to the small-appliance branch-circuit load, 3 volt-amperes per square foot general load, the nameplate rating of all appliances and motors, and air-conditioning or space heating loads.

TABLE 220-32 Optional Calculation—Demand Factors for Three or More Multifamily Dwelling Units

Number of Dwelling Units	*Demand Factor Percent*
3–5	45
6–7	44
8–10	43
11	42

TABLE 220-32 (continued)

Number of Dwelling Units	*Demand Factor Percent*
12–13	41
14–15	40
16–17	39
18–20	38
21	37
22–23	36
24–25	35
26–27	34
28–30	33
31	32
32–33	31
34–36	30
37–38	29
39–42	28
43–45	27
46–50	26
51–55	25
56–61	24
62 and over	23

220-33 Optional Calculation—Two Dwelling Units

220-34 Optional Method—Schools

Refer to Table 220-34.

220-35 Optional Calculations for Additional Loads to Existing Installations

Actual kVA readings can be used if the maximum readings are known for at least 1 year, the existing demand multiplied by 125% and the new loads are not larger than the wire capacity, and proper feeder and service overcurrent protection are provided.

TABLE 220-34 Optional Method—Demand Factors for Feeders and Service-Entrance Conductors for Schools

Connected Load Volt-amperes per Square Foot	*Demand Factors Percent*
Connected load up to and including 3, plus	100
Connected load over 3 and including 20, plus	75
Connected load over 20 at	25

D. Method for Computing Farm Loads

220-40 Farm Loads—Buildings and Other Loads

220-41 Farm Loads—Total

Note: Examples for the calculations referred to in Article 220 are shown in Part B of Chapter 9 of the *NEC*®. They are shown in the same location in this book for correlation.

ARTICLE 225 OUTSIDE BRANCH CIRCUITS AND FEEDERS

225-1 Scope

This article covers feeders and branch circuits located outside buildings.

225-2 Other Articles

The following list refers to other articles in the Code which are pertinent to outside branch circuits and feeders.

	Article
Branch Circuits	210
Class 1, Class 2, and Class 3 Remote-Control, Signaling, and Power-Limited Circuits	725
Communication Circuits	800
Community Antenna Television and Radio Distribution Systems	820
Conductors	310
Electrically Driven or Controlled Irrigation Machines	675
Electric Signs and Outline Lighting	600
Feeders	215
Fire Protective Signaling Systems	760
Fixed Outdoor Electric De-icing and Snow-Melting Equipment	426
Fixtures	410
Floating Buildings	553
Grounding	250
Hazardous (Classified) Locations	500
Hazardous (Classified) Locations, Specific	510
Marinas and Boatyards	555
Messenger Supported Wiring	321
Open Wiring on Insulators	320
Over 600 Volts, General	710
Overcurrent Protection	240
Radio and Television Equipment	810
Services	230
Solar Photovoltaic Systems	690
Swimming Pools, Fountains, and Similar Installations	680
Use and Identification of Grounded Conductors	200

225-3 Calculation of Load

The same as in Article 220.

225-4 Conductor Covering

Conductors must be insulated within 10 ft of a building. Thermoplastic or rubber insulation must be used in raceways. An exception is made for equipment grounding conductors.

225-5 Size of Conductors

Refer to Tables 310-16 through 310-31.

225-6 Minimum Size of Conductor

(a) Overhead Spans

600 V or less, up to 50 ft: No. 10 copper, No. 8 aluminum

600 V or less, over 50 ft: No. 8 copper, No. 6 aluminum

More than 600 V: No. 6 copper, No. 4 aluminum for open conductors; No. 8 copper, No. 6 aluminum for cable

(b) No. 12 or Larger for Festoon Lighting except where messenger wires support them

225-7 Lighting Equipment on Poles or Other Structures

225-8 Disconnection

Refer to Article 240.

225-9 Overcurrent Protection

Refer to Section 210-20 and Article 240.

225-10 Wiring on Buildings

225-11 Circuit Exits and Entrances

Refer to Sections 240-43, 240-52, and 240-54.

225-12 Open Conductor Supports

225-13 Festoon Supports

225-14 Open Conductor Spacing

225-15 Supports over Buildings

Refer to Section 230-29.

225-16 Point of Attachment to Buildings

Refer to Section 230-26.

225-17 Means of Attachment to Buildings

Refer to Section 230-27.

225-18 Clearance from Ground for Open Conductors Not Over 600 Volts Nominal:

10 ft: above finished grade: 150 V to ground.
12 ft: over residential driveways and commercial areas not subject to truck traffic: 300 V to ground limitation.
15 ft: same as 12 ft above: 300 V to ground.
18 ft: above streets, driveways, etc. subject to truck traffic as well as land used by vehicles such as forest, grazing, etc.

225-19 Clearances for Conductors of Not Over 600 Volts, Nominal

(a) Over Roofs—Vertical or Diagonal

10 ft: conductors not insulated for operating voltage.
3 ft: fully insulated conductors
15 ft: accessible to pedestrians—uninsulated conductors
8 ft: accessible to pedestrians—insulated conductors
18 ft: accessible to vehicular traffic
3 ft: voltage between conductors not more than 300 V and roof slope is maximum of 4 in. in 12 in.
18 inches: voltage between conductors not more than 300 V and do not pass more than 4 ft of an overhang and are terminated in approved support or raceway through the roof

(b) From Nonbuilding or Nonbridge Structures. Clearances in all directions to be a minimum of 5 ft for uninsulated conductors and 3 ft for insulated conductors.

(c) Horizontal Clearances

(d) Final Spans. Those may be attached to a building but must clear windows, fire escapes, and the like by 3 ft. If above the top level of a window then it can be reduced to less than 3 feet.

(e) Zone for Fire Ladders. Allow for fire ladders—at least a 6-ft-wide space.

225-20 Mechanical Protection of Conductors

Refer to Section 230-50.

225-21 Multiconductor Cables on Exterior Surfaces of Buildings

Refer to Section 230-51.

225-22 Raceways on Exterior Surfaces of Buildings

225-23 Underground Circuits

Refer to Section 300-5.

225-24 Outdoor Lampholders

225-25 Location of Outdoor Lampholders

225-26 Live Vegetation

ARTICLE 230
SERVICES

230-1 Scope

This article describes requirements for service conductors and equipment for control and protection of services. Diagram 230-1 on page 70-62 of the *NEC*® describes where in Article 230 different parts of the service are described.

A. General

230-2 Number of Services

A building normally can have only one service. If more than one is permitted as a result of the exceptions provided, then a directory of all services must be placed at each service. More than one service is permitted as follows:

(a) For a fire pump if required.

(b) For emergency or standby services.

(c) In multiple-occupancy buildings where there is no room for each tenant to have access to the service, with permission, more than one set of service conductors can be tapped from one service drop or service lateral.

(d) As a result of capacity requirements when the capacity exceeds 3000 A at a voltage not more than 600 V, or the utility company requires it as a result of the load.

(e) If the building is very large, with special permission.

(f) When different voltages, frequencies, etc., are required.

(g) When underground conductors are sized at least 1/0 and are connected at the supply but not at the load and service equipment for use only for the purpose of Section 230-40, Exception No. 2.

230-3 One Building or Other Structure Not Supplied through Another

Service conductors cannot pass through another building. Refer to Section 230-44 for conditions where conductors are considered outside a building, such as concrete encased.

230-6 Conductors Considered Outside of Building

If conductors have a cover of at least 2 in. of concrete under a building or are encased in at least 2 in. of concrete or are installed in a transformer vault as per Article 450 Part C, they are treated as being outside the building.

230-7 Other Conductors in Raceway or Cable

230-8 Raceway Seal

230-9 Clearance from Building Openings

If installed as open conductors or multiconductor cable without an outer jacket, clearance of at least 3 ft is required from windows, doors, porches, fire escapes, and the like. Service conductors are not permitted underneath openings through which materials can be moved or obstructing these openings.

B. Overhead Service—Drop Conductors

230-21 Overhead Supply

Definition of service drop.

230-22 Insulation or Covering

Insulation must be either thermoplastic or thermosetting and be capable of being exposed to the atmosphere and other conditions without leakage current.

230-23 Size and Rating

The minimum size generally should be No. 8 copper or No. 6 aluminum or copper-clad aluminum.

230-24 Clearances

(a) Eight feet is generally the clearance required above roofs with a nominal voltage of 600 V. This is reduced to 3 ft with a voltage of 300 V and a roof slope of 4 in. in 12 in. or more. It is also reduced to 18 in. with a nominal voltage of 300 V if only up to 4 ft of service drop conductors pass over the roof and the conductors end on a support or raceway. Where there is traffic above a roof surface use requirements of Section 230-24(b).

(b) The clearances above the ground vary for conductors with a nominal voltage of 600 V. They are:

> 10 ft: voltage of 150 V to ground, service entrance to buildings accessible to pedestrians.
> 15 ft: at residential property—no trucks. This is reduced to 12 ft when the voltage does not exceed 300 V.
> 18 ft: over public streets. Private property is included if traveled with commercial vehicles.

(c) Refer to Section 230-9 for clearances from building openings.

(d) Refer to Section 680-8 for clearances from swimming pools.

230-26 Point of Attachment

A minimum clearance of 10 ft is required. Compliance with Section 230-24 is required.

230-27 Means of Attachment

230-28 Service Masts as Support

230-29 Supports over Buildings

C. Underground Service—Lateral Conductors

230-30 Insulation

Generally, the voltage used determines the voltage rating of the insulation. There are some exceptions for grounded conductors of bare wire and aluminum or copper-clad aluminum cable assemblies.

230-31 Size and Rating

The conductors must be large enough to carry the load in accordance with Article 220. No smaller than No. 8 for copper and No. 6 for aluminum or copper-clad aluminum. An exception is made where the service supplies only a single load on a single branch circuit. The grounded conductor must not be sized less than required in Section 250-23(b).

230-32 Protection Against Damage

D. Service-Entrance Conductors

230-40 Number of Service Entrance Conductor Sets

Generally, a service drop or lateral can only supply one set of service conductors. However, one set of service conductors can supply each occupancy or a group of occupancies in a multiple occupancy building. A second exception for separate enclosures is noted.

230-41 Insulation of Service-Entrance Conductors

Generally, if the conductors are on or enter a building, they should be insulated. Exceptions are made for grounded conductors of bare copper wire and aluminum or copper-clad aluminum cable assemblies in special cases.

230-42 Size and Rating

Generally, they are required to be large enough to carry the load. A minimum of 100 A three-wire is required for a one-family dwelling with either six or more two-wire branch circuits or a load of at least 10 kVA. A minimum of 60 A is required for other loads with three exceptions. The grounded conductor must comply with Section 250-23(b).

230-43 Wiring Methods for 600 Volts, Nominal or Less

Only the following methods are permitted: Open wiring on insulators, rigid metal conduit, intermediate metal conduit, EMT, service entrance cables, wireways, busways, auxiliary gutters, rigid NMC, cablebus, MC cable, mineral-insulated, metal-sheathed cable and flexible metal conduit with certain restrictions. To support cables, a cable tray system may be used.

230-46 Unspliced Conductors

230-49 Protection against Damage—Underground

230-50 Protection of Open Conductors and Cables against Damage—Above Ground

230-51 Mounting Supports

230-52 Individual Conductors Entering Buildings or Other Structures

230-53 Raceways to Drain

230-54 Connections at Service Head

Connections have to be made raintight with a raintight head or with a gooseneck properly taped. The heads or goosenecks must be above the point where the conductors are attached to the building and must be securely attached. Drip loops must be constructed to prevent entrance of moisture.

230-55 Termination at Service Equipment

230-56 Service-Entrance Conductor with the Higher Voltage to Ground

E. Service Equipment—General

230-62 Service Equipment—Enclosed or Guarded

Live parts must be enclosed or installed in switchboard or similar equipment as stated in Sections 110-17 and 110-18.

230-63 Grounding and Bonding

230-64 Working Space

230-65 Available Short Circuit

F. Service Equipment—Disconnecting Means

230-70 General

There must be a way to disconnect all conductors in the building from the service-entrance conductors. It must be located inside or outside the structure nearest the point of entrance of the service conductors, be readily accessible, have proper markings, and be suitable for its use.

230-71 Maximum Number of Disconnects

The provision for disconnecting each service (Section 230-2) or the service entrance conductors (Section 230-40, Exception No. 1) can consist of no more than six switches or six circuit breakers. Single-pole units can be used for multiwire circuits, one pole for each ungrounded conductor. They must be tied together as a multipole disconnect and will then be counted as one disconnect. An exception is made for the control circuit of a ground-fault protection system.

230-72 Grouping of Disconnects

All disconnects are to be grouped together. Exceptions are for services mentioned in Section 230-2 and when a switch is used for a fire pump. The service disconnects must be located near the point of entry to the building and must be readily accessible. Where multiple occupancies are present, each occupant must have access to his or her own disconnect. An exception is made to this latter requirement for certain management conditions.

230-74 Simultaneous Opening of Poles

230-75 Disconnection of Grounded Conductor

230-76 Manually or Power Operable

230-77 Indicating

230-78 External Operable

The disconnect must be operable from the outside without the operator coming into contact with energized parts.

230-79 Rating of Disconnect

In general, the service disconnect must be sized to carry the calculated load. There are special cases where a minimum size is required. They are:

15 A: a single branch-circuit load
30 A: up to two, two-wire branch circuits
100 A, three-wire: one-family dwelling with six or more two-wire branch circuits or calculated load is 10 kW or more
60 A: all other cases

230-80 Combined Rating of Disconnects

If more than one service switch is used, their combined rating must be at least the rating shown in Section 230-79.

230-81 Connection to Terminals

230-82 Equipment Connected to the Supply Side of Service Disconnect

Among the pieces of equipment allowed to be connected to the supply side of a service switch are: current-limiting devices, meters, disconnecting devices used as service equipment, meters, instrument transformers, surge protective devices, emergency circuits, fire and sprinkler alarms, fire pumps and interconnected electric production sources. Some of these items require separate protection and disconnects. Refer to the *NEC®* for a complete description.

230-83 Transfer Equipment

230-84 More Than One Building or Other Structure

Every building must have its own disconnecting means. The Code provides an exception under certain conditions for large capacity, multibuilding, industrial installations and those permitted in Article 695.

G. Service Equipment—Overcurrent Protection

230-90 Where Required

(a) Every ungrounded conductor must have an overcurrent device. It must normally not be set higher than the rating of the conductors. There are four exceptions to this and they include: motors; where no exact size exists; six fuses or circuit breakers is the limit for consideration as a service overcurrent device; fire pumps under certain conditions.

(b) No overcurrent device is to be placed in an ungrounded conductor.

230-91 Location of Overload Protection

Each occupant of a multiple dwelling must have access to his or her own overcurrent protection. If there is more than one building under single management, the ungrounded conductors to each building must have an overcurrent device in that building, or in another building provided that it is accessible to each occupant of the building served.

230-92 Locked Service Overcurrent Devices

230-93 Protection of Specific Circuits

230-94 Relative Location of Overcurrent Devices and Other Service Equipment

Some of the items allowed ahead of the overcurrent device are: service switch, surge protectors, emergency supply signaling systems, fire pump, meters, and power-operable service equipment controls

230-95 Ground-Fault Protection of Equipment

This is required for all services that are 150 V to ground up to 600 V phase to phase, grounded wye, with service switches 1000 A or more. The rest of this section contains information about the setting of these devices, the use of switches and fuses, and performance testing. An exception is allowed for continuous industrial processes where a non-orderly shutdown would be hazardous and for fire pumps

H. Services Exceeding 600 Volts Nominal

230-200 General

230-201 Service Conductors

230-202 Service Entrance Conductors

230-203 Warning Signs

230-204 Isolating Switches

230-205 Disconnecting Means

230-206 Overcurrent Devices as Disconnecting Means

230-207 Equipment in Secondaries

230-208 Overcurrent Protection Requirements

230-209 Surge Arresters (Lighting Arresters)

230-210 Service Equipment—General Provisions

230-211 Metal-Enclosed Switchgear

ARTICLE 240
OVERCURRENT PROTECTION

240-1 Scope

Parts A through G give requirements for circuits of up to 600 V.

A. General

240-2 Protection of Equipment

Equipment must be protected according to the following articles.

	Article
Air-Conditioning and Refrigerating Equipment	440
Appliances	422
Branch Circuits	210
Capacitors	460
Class 1, Class 2, and Class 3 Remote-Control, Signaling, and Power-Limited Circuits	725
Closed-Loop and Programmed Power Distribution System	780
Cranes and Hoists	610
Electric Signs and Outline Lighting	600
Electric Welders	630
Electrolytic Cells	668
Elevators, Dumbwaiters, Escalators, and Moving Walks	620

	Article
Emergency Systems	700
Fire Protective Signaling Systems	760
Fixed Electric Heating Equipment for Pipelines and Vessels	427
Fixed Electric Space Heating Equipment	424
Fixed Outdoor Electric De-icing and Snow-Melting Equipment	426
Generators	445
Induction and Dielectric Heating Equipment	665
Industrial Machinery	670
Motion Picture and Television Studios and Similar Locations	530
Motors, Motor Circuits, and Controllers	430
Organs	650
Over 600 Volts, Nominal—General	710
Places of Assembly	518
Services	230
Solar Photovoltaic Systems	690
Sound-Recording and Similar Equipment	640
Switchboards and Panelboards	384
Theaters and Similar Locations	520
Transformers and Transformer Vaults	450
X-Ray Equipment	517 660

240-3 Protection of Conductors Other Than Flexible Cords and Fixture Wires

When sizing overcurrent devices, refer to Tables 310-16 through 310-31 for ampacities of conductors. In general, protect according to these ampacities. There are eight exceptions: using the next-higher-rated available device, tap conductors as permitted, motor circuits, remote control circuits, transformer secondary circuits under certain conditions, capacitor circuits, welders circuits, and in case of undue hazard for loss of power. In each case there are special requirements that must be met.

240-4 Protection of Fixture Wires and Cords

240-6 Standard Ampere Ratings

The standard ratings for fuses and circuit breakers are: 15, 20, 25, 30, 35, 40, 45, 50, 60, 70, 80, 90, 100, 110, 125, 150, 175, 200, 225, 250, 300, 350, 400, 450, 500, 600, 700, 800, 1000, 1200, 1600, 2000, 2500, 3000, 4000, 5000, and 6000 A. Fuses are also rated at 1, 3, 6, 10, and 601 A.

240-8 Fuses or Circuit Breakers in Parallel

240-9 Thermal Devices

240-10 Supplementary Overcurrent Protection

240-11 Definition of Current-Limiting Overcurrent Protective Device

240-12 Electrical System Coordination

If an orderly shutdown is required to reduce hazards to equipment and personnel, the following methods can be used; coordinated short-circuit protection and/or overload indication.

B. Location

240-20 Ungrounded Conductors

An overcurrent device (fuse or circuit breaker) has to be connected in series with each ungrounded conductor. An overcurrent relay with a current transformer is allowed. Generally, a circuit breaker has to open all ungrounded conductors. Single-pole circuit breakers are permitted under certain conditions listed in this section. In a closed-loop power distribution system, listed devices can be used instead of fuses or circuit breakers.

240-21 Location in Circuit

In general, the overcurrent device must be located at the supply to the conductors. There are some exceptions:

Exception No. 1. When a circuit is tapped from another conductor and the size of protection for the original supply is proper for the tap, the tap does not require protection.

Exception No. 2. When the tap is not longer than 10 ft, it does not require protection if the tap is also rated not less than the loads it will supply, mechanically protected, and ends at the first enclosure for the load.

Exception No. 3. When the tap is not longer than 25 ft, it does not require protection if the ampacity of the tap is at least one-third the rating of the feeder or overcurrent protection it was tapped from, ends in a single overcurrent device rated for the tap, and is mechanically protected.

Exception No. 4. Service entrance conductors as per Section 230-91.

Exception No. 5. Branch-circuit taps when installed as per Sections 210-19, 210-20, and 210-21.

Exception No. 6. Motor circuit taps when installed as per Sections 430-28 and 430-53.

Exception No. 7. Busways when installed as per Sections 364-10 through 364-14.

Exception No. 8. Transformer Taps: similar to the 25-ft tap (Exception No. 3). No protection is required at the tap for the transformer if both primary and secondary wires are not longer than 25 ft combined and both ratings (including transformer ratio for secondary) are not larger than one-third the rating of the circuit being tapped, the tap is mechanically protected, and the tap ends in a single overcurrent device.

Exception No. 9. Generator conductors as per Section 445-5.

Exception No. 10. An additional exception is made for manufacturing installations with bays over 35 ft in height. In this case no protection is required for the tap if the horizontal length is not longer than 25 ft, with the overall length not longer than 100 ft. All the rules of the 25-ft tap rule (Exception No. 3) apply, and in addition, the tap conductors must be at least No. 6 copper or No. 4 aluminum and cannot go through floors, walls, or ceilings with the tap at least 30 ft from the floor.

Exception No. 11. Discusses transformer secondary conductors of separately derived systems.

240-22 Grounded Conductors

No overcurrent device should be placed in series with a grounded conductor unless it simultaneously opens all other conductors of the circuit or when required by Sections 430-36 and 430-37.

240-23 Change in Size of Grounded Conductor

240-24 Location in or on Premises

Overcurrent devices must be readily accessible and each occupant must have access to the ones protecting the conductors for his or her occupancy. The overcurrent devices must not be exposed to physical damage and must not be located near easily ignitable material. Refer to the *NEC*® for certain exceptions.

C. Enclosures

240-30 General

240-32 Damp or Wet Locations

240-33 Vertical Position

D. Disconnecting Means

240-40 Disconnecting Means for Fuses and Thermal Cutouts

In general, the disconnection means must be provided on the supply side of the overcurrent device. This does not hold true for service current-limiting devices as per Section 230-82 or single disconnecting devices for multiple sets of fuses as per Section 430-112 (generators) and Section 424-22 (fixed electric space heating).

240-41 Arcing or Suddenly Moving Parts

E. Plug Fuses, Fuseholders, and Adapters

240-50 General

These are not permitted in circuits where the voltage between conductors is more than 125 V except with a grounded neutral and not more than 150 V to ground.

240-51 Edison-Base Fuses

240-52 Edison-Base Fuseholders

240-53 Type S Fuses

240-54 Type S Fuses, Adapters and Fuseholders

F. Cartridge Fuses and Fuseholders

240-60 General

These are not permitted in circuits operating at over 300 V between conductors if rated 300 V, unless the circuits have a grounded neutral and operate at not more than 300 V to ground. The holders must prevent interchangeability where a fuse can be put into a circuit of lower ampere rating or higher voltage rating. All fuses must be marked, indicating the current, voltage, and interrupting rating, if it is current limiting, and the manufacturer's name and trademark. The interrupting rating is not required when they are used for supplementary protection.

240-61 Classification

G. Circuit Breakers

240-80 Method of Operation

Normally, they must be trip free and capable of manual operation in addition to other normal means, such as electrical or pneumatic operation.

240-81 Indicating

Must indicate on or off—on is up position if mounted vertically.

240-82 Nontamperable

240-83 Marking

They must all be properly marked. When properly used as a switch, they must be approved for switching duty and marked SWD.

H. Overcurrent Protection Over 600 Volts, Nominal

240-100 Feeders

240-101 Branch Circuits

ARTICLE 250
GROUNDING

A. General

250-1 Scope

Generally gives requirements for grounding.

250-2 Application of Other Articles

The following other articles have special grounding requirements:

	Article	*Section*
Agricultural Buildings		547-8
Appliances		422-16
Branch Circuits		210-5 210-6 210-7
Cablebus		365-9
Circuits and Equipment Operating at Less Than 50 Volts	720	
Class 1, Class 2, and Class 3 Circuits		725-20 725-42
Closed-Loop and Programmed Power Distribution		780-3 780-4(a)
Communications Circuits	800	
Community Antenna Television and Radio Distribution Systems		820-7 820-22 820-23
Conductors	310	
Conductors (Grounded)	200	
Cranes and Hoists	610	
Data Processing Systems		645-4
Electrically Driven or Controlled Irrigation Machines		675-11(c) 675-12 675-13 675-14 675-15
Electric Signs and Outline Lighting	600	
Electrolytic Cells	668	
Elevators, Dumbwaiters, Escalators, and	620	

	Article	Section
Moving Walks		
Fire Protective Signaling Systems		760-6
Fixed Electric Heating Equipment for Pipelines and Vessels		427-21 427-29 427-48
Fixed Electric Space Heating Equipment		424-14
Fixed Outdoor Electric De-icing and Snow-Melting Equipment		426-27
Fixtures and Lighting Equipment		410-17 410-18 410-19 410-21 410-105(b)
Flexible Cords		400-22 400-23
Floating Buildings		553-8 553-10 553-11
Grounding-Type Receptacles (Outlets)		210-7
Hazardous (Classified) Locations	500-517	
Health Care Facilities	517	
Induction and Dielectric Heating Equipment	665	
Industrial Machinery	670	
Lighting Fixtures, Lampholders, Lamp Receptacles, and Rosettes	410	
Marinas and Boatyards		555-7
Mobile Homes and Mobile Home Parks	550	
Motion Picture and Television Studios		530-20 530-66

	Article	Section
and Similar Locations		
Motors, Motor Circuits, and Controllers	430	
Organs	650	
Outlet, Device, Pull and Junction Boxes, Conduit Bodies, and Fittings		370-4 370-15
Over 600 Volts, General		710-3(b)(1)
Panelboards		384-27
Radio and Television Equipment	810	
Receptacles and Attachment Plugs		410-58
Recreational Vehicles and Recreational Vehicle Parks	551	
Services	230	
Service Equipment		230-63
Solar Photovoltaic Systems		690-41 690-42 690-43 690-44
Sound-Recording and Similar Equipment		640-4
Swimming Pools, Fountains and Similar Installations	680	
Switchboards and Panelboards		384-3(c) 384-11
Switches		380-12
Theaters and Similar Locations		520-81
Transformers and Transformer Vaults		450-10
X-Ray Equipment	660	517-151

B. Circuit and System Grounding

250-3 Direct-Current Systems

250-5 Alternating-Current Circuits and Systems to Be Grounded

The following circuits and systems must be grounded. Others may be grounded if desired.

(a) Alternating-current circuits of less than 50 V must be grounded if supplied by transformer systems of more than 150 V to ground or by ungrounded transformer systems. All outdoor circuits must be grounded.

(b) Alternating-current circuits between 50 and 1000 V of the following types must be grounded:

1. Systems of up to 150 V to ground from an ungrounded conductor
2. Systems of 480/277 V, three-phase, four-wire with a neutral circuit conductor
3. Three-phase 120/240-V delta systems with a neutral tap on one phase
4. Uninsulated service conductor as per Section 230-4

There are a number of exceptions and the reader is referred to Section 250-5(b), Exception Nos. 1 through 5.

(c) Alternating-Current Systems 1 kV and Over

(d) Separately Derived Systems. If the source is separately derived, has no connection to another source, or is grounded and required to be grounded, it must be grounded as required by Section 250-26.

250-6 Portable and Vehicle-Mounted Generators

250-7 Circuits Not to Be Grounded

Those specified in Article 517 and electric cranes used in areas of Class III over combustible fibers.

C. Location of System Grounding Connections

250-12 Objectionable Current over Grounding Conductors

250-22 Point of Connection for Direct-Current Systems

250-23 Grounding Service-Supplied Alternating-Current Systems

As required, each service must have a grounding electrode conductor connected to a grounding electrode. The reader should become familiar with the requirements of this article in the *NEC*®.

250-24 Two or More Buildings or Structures Supplied from a Common Service

Each building must have a grounding electrode (refer to Part H) connected to the building disconnecting devices metal enclosure. In a grounded system, the electrode must also connect to the grounded conductor of the ac system on the supply side of the building disconnecting device. There are two exceptions to this.

250-25 Conductor to Be Grounded—Alternating-Current Systems

One conductor must be grounded in a two-wire single-phase system. The neutral conductor is grounded in a three-wire single-phase system and a multiphase system where one phase is used as a three-wire single-phase system. The common conductor is grounded in a multiphase system with one wire common to all phases. A phase conductor is grounded in a multiphase system requiring it.

250-26 Grounding Separately Derived Alternating-Current Systems

D. Enclosure Grounding

250-32 Service Raceways and Enclosures

These metal enclosures must be grounded.

250-33 Other Conductor Enclosures

These metal enclosures must be grounded. Note two exceptions for open wire: knob and tubing and nonmetallic-sheathed cable, and enclosures used to physically protect cable assemblies.

E. Equipment Grounding

250-42 Equipment Fastened in Place or Connected by Permanent Wiring Methods (Fixed)

Metal enclosures must be grounded if located in a wet or damp location and not isolated, if they can be touched by people and are 8 ft or less vertically and 5 ft or less horizontally to ground or a grounded object, if in contact with metal, if in a hazardous location, if metal-clad type of wiring is used under certain conditions, and if the voltage is greater than 150 V to ground. There are three exceptions to the last case.

250-43 Fastened in Place or Connected by Permanent Wiring Methods (Fixed)—Specific

All exposed metal parts that do not conduct current of the following equipment must be grounded: switchboard frames and structures except two-wire dc where insulated; organs; motor frames and enclosures; elevators and cranes; all electric equipment in garages, theaters, and motion picture studios except pendant lampholders of 150 V or less; electric signs except when insulated from other conducto and ground and accessible only to qualified persons; motion picture equipment; Class 1, 2, and 3 circuits where required; lighting fixtures as per Article 410.

250-44 Nonelectric Equipment

The metal parts of this equipment must be grounded: cranes; elevator cars of nonelectric type; electric elevators, metal partitions enclosing conductors of 1 kV and over to ground; mobile homes and recreational vehicles per Articles 550 and 551.

250-45 Equipment Connected by Cord and Plug

There are areas where exposed metal parts (noncurrent-carrying) must be grounded even though connected by cord and plug. This is true of hazardous locations and circuits over 150 V to ground; three exceptions are motors when guarded, electrically heated appliances with special exemptions and insulation to ground and listed information processing and office equipment under certain conditions. In a residence the following items are required to have equipment grounding: refrigerators, freezers, and air conditioners; clothes washing and drying equipment; dishwashing machines; sump pumps and electrical aquarium equipment; hand-held motor-operated tools, motor-operated hedge clippers, lawn mowers, snow blowers, wet scrubbers, etc.; and portable handlamps. If the appliance has double insulation and is so listed, equipment grounding is not necessary. In other than residences, the list is the same as residences, with the addition of cord- and plug-connected appliances in damp or wet locations and portable headlamps, electronic computer data processing equipment, tools used in wet and conductive locations. The same exception as in residences is in effect, with an additional exception for tools in wet and conductive locations if supplied through an isolating transformer with a secondary ungrounded and not over 50 V.

250-46 Spacing from Lightning Rods

F. Methods of Grounding

250-50 Equipment Grounding Conductor Connectors

250-51 Effective Grounding Path

250-53 Grounding Path to Grounding Electrode at Services

A grounded item (equipment grounding conductors, service equipment enclosures, and the grounded service conductors) must be connected to the grounding electrode.

240-54 Common Grounding Electrode

Where the ac system is grounded, the system and equipment must be grounded to the same electrode or electrodes bonded together

250-55 Underground Service Cable

The metal sheath of an underground cable system or its metal conduit does not have to be grounded at the building, assuming that it is a continuous system.

250-56 Short Sections of Raceway

250-57 Equipment Fastened in Place or Connected by Permanent Wiring Methods (Fixed)—Grounding

250-58 Equipment Considered Effectively Grounded

(a) This is true when it is electrically connected to a supporting metal rack or structure that is properly grounded. The building's structural steel is not considered an effective grounding method.

(b) Metal Car Frames

250-59 Cord- and Plug-Connected Equipment

250-60 Frames of Ranges and Clothes Dryers

250-61 Use of Grounded Circuit Conductor for Grounding Equipment

(a) Generally, a grounded circuit conductor can be used to ground equipment on the supply side of the service disconnect.

(b) Generally, a grounded circuit conductor cannot be used to ground equipment on the load side of the service disconnect. There are four exceptions to this:

1. As indicated in Section 250-60 for ranges, wall-mounted ovens, etc.
2. For separate buildings as indicated in Section 250-24.
3. Grounding meter enclosures if no service ground-fault protection is used and the meter is near the service switch.
4. In accordance with Sections 710-72(e)(1) and 710-74.

250-62 Multiple Circuit Connections

G. Bonding

250-70 General

Bonding must be provided to make sure there is proper electrical continuity in the grounding system.

250-71 Service Equipment

All service equipment must be bonded. All other systems must be bonded to the electrical system. (e.g., cable TV)

250-72 Methods of Bonding Service Equipment

There are five approved methods:

(a) Pressure connectors, clamps, etc., for the service conductor

(b) Threaded couplings for rigid metal conduit and intermediate metal conduit

(c) Threadless couplings and connectors for rigid and intermediate metal conduit and electrical metallic tubing

(d) Bonding jumpers around knockouts

(e) Other devices

250-73 Metal Armor or Tape of Service Cable

250-74 Connecting Receptacle Grounding Terminal to Box

Generally, a bonding jumper must be used. There are four exceptions:

1. If the box is service mounted and the yoke makes good electrical contact with the box. There are restrictions on cover-mounted receptacles.
2. Where the receptacle is listed as such with special yokes and screws.
3. Floor boxes so listed.
4. Where there is a requirement for the reduction of electrical noise, an insulated grounding conductor can be used. It is run with the circuit conductors.

250-75 Bonding Other Enclosures

All items that will be used as grounding conductors must be bonded.

250-76 Bonding for Over 250 Volts

250-77 Bonding Loosely Jointed Metal Raceways

250-78 Bonding in Hazardous (Classified) Locations

All items in a hazardous (classified) location must be bonded as required by Section 250-72(b)–(e), regardless of the voltage.

250-79 Main and Equipment Bonding Jumpers

250-80 Bonding of Piping Systems

H. Grounding Electrode System

250-81 Grounding Electrode System

The following four items if they exist must be bonded together. Any one of them can be considered the grounding electrode.

(a) Metal Underground Water Pipe. This must be underground for at least 10 ft and an additional electrode is required.

(b) Metal Frame of the Building Effectively Grounded

(c) Concrete—Encased Electrode. The electrode must be at least 20 ft of No. 4 wire or 20 ft of steel reinforcing rods at least ½ in. in diameter. It must be encased in a minimum of 2 in. of concrete near the bottom of the foundation.

(d) Ground Ring

250-83 Made and Other Electrodes

Other methods may be used when none of the ones in Section 250-82 are available. These are metal underground gas piping systems, other local metal underground systems or structures, rod and pipe electrodes, and plate electrodes. The reader is referred to this section in the *NEC*® for complete details.

250-84 Resistance of Made Electrodes

250-86 Use of Lightning Rods

They are not to be used for grounding electrodes.

J. Grounding Conductors

250-91 Material

(a) Grounding Electrode Conductor. The material is to be solid or stranded copper, aluminum, or copper-clad aluminum. It can be bare, covered, or insulated and must not contain a splice. There are two exceptions where splices are permitted.

1. In busbars.
2. Taps are permitted where there is more than one service enclosure.

(b) Types of Equipment Grounding Conductors. The following may be used for equipment grounding conductors.

1. Copper or other corrosion-resistant conductor. As with the grounding electrode, it can be solid or stranded, and bare, covered, or insulated.
2. Rigid metal conduit.
3. Intermediate metal conduit.
4. Electrical metallic tubing.
5. Flexible metal conduit (approved for grounding).
6. Armor of Type AC cable.
7. The sheath of MI cable.
8. The sheath of MC cable.
9. Cable trays.
10. Other metal raceways approved for this purpose. Flexible metal conduit and tubing are allowed if the length is not more than 6 ft, the circuit protection does not exceed 20 A, and terminations are approved for grounding. Liquidtight flexible metal conduit is allowed in sizes not exceeding 1¼ in., not longer than

6 ft, terminations are approved for grounding and overcurrent devices are not more than 20 A for 3⁄8- and 1⁄2-in. sizes and not more than 60 A for 3⁄4- and 1 1⁄4-in. sizes.

(c) Supplementary grounding conductors may be used.

250-92 Installation

(a) Grounding Electrode Conductor. If it is No. 4 copper or aluminum or larger, it must be protected if it is subject to physical damage that is severe. Number 6 wires, if fastened to the building and free from physical damage, do not need protection; if not, they must be protected in the same manner as wires smaller than No. 6. Wires smaller than No. 6 must be enclosed in either rigid metal conduit, intermediate metal conduit, rigid nonmetallic conduit, electrical metallic tubing, or cable armor. In all cases above, the wire or enclosure must be fastened to the surface it is running on. Aluminum or copper-clad aluminum cannot be used in corrosive areas.

(b) Enclosures for Grounding Electrode Conductors. A complete electrical path must be ensured for metal enclosures of grounding conductors.

(c) Equipment Grounding Conductor. If it is a metal enclosure for the conductor, or the conductor, the applicable provisions of the *NEC*® must be followed. An exception is made for existing installations where no equipment grounding conductor is available for branch-circuit extensions.

250-93 Size of Direct-Current System Grounding Conductor

It cannot be smaller than the neutral conductor for a three-wire balancer set or balancer winding. It cannot be smaller than the largest conductor if other than as stated in the preceding sentence. It can never be smaller than No. 8 copper or No. 6 aluminum.

250-94 Size of Alternating-Current Grounding Electrode Conductor

These minimum sizes are given in Table 250-94. There are two exceptions, one for grounded systems and one for ungrounded systems.

250-95 Size of Equipment Grounding Conductors

These minimum sizes are given in Table 250-95. When circuit conductors are run in parallel, the equipment grounding conductor must be run in parallel and sized according to the overcurrent device rating shown in the table. The conductor never has to be larger than the circuit conductor to the equipment. Raceway, cable armor, or sheath can be used as the conductor and does not have to follow the sizes listed in Table 250-95.

250-97 Outline Lighting

250-99 Equipment Grounding Conductor Continuity

K. Grounding Conductor Connections

250-112 To Grounding Electrode

It must be accessible and provide an effective and permanent ground.

250-113 To Conductors and Equipment

Use only listed connectors and not ones that depend on solder.

250-114 Continuity and Attachment of Branch-Circuit Equipment Grounding Conductors to Boxes

Table 250-94 Grounding Electrode Conductor for AC Systems

Size of Largest Service-Entrance Conductor or Equivalent Area for Parallel Conductors		*Size of Grounding Electrode Conductor*	
Copper	*Aluminum or Copper-Clad Aluminum*	*Copper*	*Aluminum or Copper-Clad Aluminum**
2 or smaller	0 or smaller	8	6
1 or 0	2/0 or 3/0	6	4
2/0 or 3/0	4/0 or 250 MCM	4	2
Over 3/0 through 350 MCM	Over 250 MCM through 500 MCM	2	0
Over 350 MCM through 600 MCM	Over 500 MCM through 900 MCM	0	3/0
Over 600 MCM through 1100 MCM	Over 900 MCM through 1750 MCM	2/0	4/0
Over 1100 MCM	Over 1750 MCM	3/0	250 MCM

Where there are no service-entrance conductors, the grounding electrode conductor size shall be determined by the equivalent size of the largest service-entrance conductor required for the load to be served.

See Section 250-23(b).

* See installation restrictions in Section 250-92(a).

Table 250-95 Minimum Size Equipment Grounding Conductors for Grounding Raceway and Equipment

Rating or Setting of Automatic Overcurrent Device in Circuit Ahead of Equipment, Conduit, etc., Not Exceeding (Amperes):	*Size*	
	Copper Wire No.	*Aluminum or Copper-Clad Aluminum Wire No.**
15	14	12
20	12	10
30	10	8
40	10	8
60	10	8
100	8	6
200	6	4
300	4	2
400	3	1
500	2	1/0
600	1	2/0
800	0	3/0
1000	2/0	4/0
1200	3/0	250 MCM
1600	4/0	350 MCM
2000	250 MCM	400 MCM
2500	350 MCM	600 MCM
3000	400 MCM	600 MCM
4000	500 MCM	800 MCM
5000	700 MCM	1200 MCM
6000	800 MCM	1200 MCM

* See installation restrictions in Section 250-92(a).

250-115 Connection to Electrodes

250-117 Protection of Attachment

250-118 Clean Surfaces

L. Instrument Transformers, Relays, etc.

250-121 Instrument Transformer Circuits

250-122 Instrument Transformer Cases

250-123 Cases of Instruments, Meters, and Relays—Operating at Less Than 1000 Volts

250-124 Cases of Instruments, Meters and Relays—Operating Voltage 1 kV and Over

250-125 Instrument Grounding Conductor

M. Grounding of Systems and Circuits of 1 kV and Over (High Voltage)

250-150 General

If these systems are grounded, they must follow all previous sections as well as this section.

250-151 Derived Neutral Systems

250-152 Solidly Grounded Neutral Systems

250-153 Impedance Grounded Neutral Systems

250-154 Grounding of Systems Supplying Portable or Mobile Equipment

250-155 Grounding of Equipment

ARTICLE 280
SURGE ARRESTERS

A. General

280-1 Scope

280-2 Definition

280-3 Number Required

280-4 Surge-Arrester Selection

B. Installation

280-11 Location

280-12 Routing of Surge-Arrester Connections

C. Connecting Surge Arresters

280-21 Installed at Services of Less Than 1000 Volts

280-22 Installed on the Load Side of Services of Less Than 1000 Volts

280-23 Circuits of 1 kV and Over—Surge-Arrester Conductors

280-24 Circuits of 1 kV and Over—Interconnections

280-25 Grounding

WIRING METHODS AND MATERIALS

ARTICLE 300
WIRING METHODS

A. General Requirements

300-1 Scope

This article applies to all wiring installations except Class 1, 2, and 3 circuits referenced in Article 725; fire protective signaling circuits referenced in Article 760; optical fiber cables referenced in Article 770; communications systems referenced in Article 800; and community antenna television and radio distribution systems referenced in Article 820. It does not apply to integral parts of equipment (e.g., motors, motor control centers, etc.)

300-2 Limitations

This chapter applies to voltages up to and including 600 V when not otherwise noted and over 600 V only when specifically mentioned in the *National Electrical Code®*.

300-3 Conductors

(a) Single Conductors

(b) Conductors of the Same Circuit. All conductors of the same circuit must be installed in the same raceway, cable, etc.

(c) Conductors of Different Systems

(1) 600 Volts, Nominal, or Less. Conductors of 600 V or less can occupy the same wiring enclosure if all conductors have insulation rated for the maximum voltage used. Refer to Section 690-4(b) for solar photovoltaic systems and to Section 725-38(a)(2) for Class 2 and Class 3 conductors.

(2) Over 600 Volts, Nominal. Conductors of over 600 V cannot be in the same wiring enclosure with those rated 600 V or less except for secondary wiring to electric discharge lamps, primary leads of electric discharge lamp ballasts, and excitation, control, relay, and ammeter conductors. Reference should be made to this section in the *NEC®* for a complete explanation.

300-4 Protection against Physical Damage

300-5 Underground Installations

(a) Minimum Cover Requirements. The cover requirements for direct buried cable or conduit are: 24 in. for direct, buried cables; 6 in. for rigid metal conduit and intermediate metal conduit, and 18 in. for rigid nonmetallic conduit and other approved raceways. When concrete encasing is required, it must be at least 2 in. thick. Exceptions to this general rule include:

1. If a 2-in. concrete pad is put over the installation, the cover may be reduced by 6 in. for other than rigid or intermediate metal conduit.
2. They do not apply if under a building slab 4 in. thick or more which extends at least 6 in. beyond the installation.

3. Use 24 in. over cover where heavy vehicular traffic is expected.

4. Residential branch circuits of 300 V or less with up to 30 A of protection can have only 12 in. of cover.

5. When access to the cable is required (e.g., splicing).

6. In airport runways 18 in. over cover can be used with cables not in raceways.

7. Less cover can be used when in solid rock and 2 in. of concrete cover.

8. Irrigation and landscape lighting systems of 30 V or less with Type UF or other identified cable can have a cover of 6 in.

(b) Grounding
(c) Underground Cables under Building
(d) Protection from Damage
(e) Splices and Taps
(f) Backfill
(g) Raceway Seals
(h) Bushing
(i) Single Conductors

300-6 Protection against Corrosion

Generally, all material used must be intended for use in the installed environment.

(a) General. Ferrous material must be protected both inside and out by a coating of corrosion-resistant material (e.g., zinc, cadmium, or enamel). Enamel cannot be used outdoors or in wet locations. A specific exception is made for threads at joints.

(b) In Concrete or in Direct Contact with the Earth. If the material is made for this purpose, it can be used.

(c) Indoor Wet Locations. The cable must be installed with at least ¼ in. of air space from the wall or supporting surface.

300-7 Raceways Exposed to Different Temperatures

300-8 Installation of Conductors with Other Systems

300-9 Grounding Metal Enclosures

300-10 Electrical Continuity of Metal Raceways and Enclosures

There must be electrical continuity between all metal raceways, cable armor, and metal enclosures.

300-11 Securing and Supporting

300-12 Mechanical Continuity—Raceways and Cables

300-13 Mechanical and Electrical Continuity—Conductors

Splices or taps are not permitted within a raceway. Exceptions to this are noted in Section 374-8 for auxiliary gutters; Section 362-6 for wireways; Section 300-15(a), Exception No. 1, for boxes and fittings; and Section 352-7 for metal surface raceways.

300-14 Length of Free Conductors at Outlets, Junctions, and Switch Points

At least 6 in. of conductors must be left at every outlet, junction, or switch point unless the conductors are not spliced or terminated at that point.

300-15 Boxes or Fittings—Where Required

(a) Box or Fitting. A box or fitting must be used at each conductor splice point, connection point or pullpoint, and outlet switch point for the connection of conduit and raceways unless access is provided at the point with a removable cover in items such as a conduit bodies, surface raceway, etc.

(b) Box Only. A box is required where cable is used except as follows:

1. For insulated outlet devices supplied by nonmetallic-sheathed cable, refer to Section 336-11.
2. Refer to Section 410-62 for rosettes.
3. When using MI cable, metal-sheathed cable with accessible fittings in straight-through splices.
4. Where cable enters or exits from a raceway used for support or physical damage protection. Fittings must be installed to protect the wire from wear.
5. When using nonmetallic-sheathed cable with a box that is secured to a structural member under certain conditions.
6. When a manufactured metallic system is used.
7. When complying with Sections 370-6(c) and 370-18 a conduit body can be used instead of a box.
8. When a device is listed for use without a box in a closed-loop power distribution system.

300-16 Raceway or Cable to Open or Concealed Wiring

300-17 Number and Size of Conductors in Raceway

In general, the number and size of conductors in a raceway must allow the dissipation of heat, easy installation, and withdrawal.

300-19 Supporting Conductors in Vertical Raceways.

Conductors must be supported at the top and bottom of vertical risers with additional support as noted in Table 300-19(a) of the *NEC*®.

300-20 Induced Currents in Metal Enclosures or Metal Raceways

The effects of induced currents in metal enclosures must be minimized. This is done by grouping all phase, neutral, and grounding conductors in one raceway. If individual conductors are used, a slot can be cut between the holes made in the metallic enclosure through which the individual conductor passes.

300-21 Spread of Fire or Products Combustion

300-22 Wiring in Ducts, Plenums, and Other Air-Handling Spaces

(a) Ducts for Dust, Loose Stock, or Vapor Removal. Wiring of any type is prohibited in these types of installations. This includes ventilation of commercial-type cooking equipment.

(b) Ducts or Plenums Used for Environmental Air. The following can be used in this type of installation: Type MI metal sheathed cable, Type MC cable, EMT flexible metallic tubing, intermediate metal conduit, or rigid metal conduit. When necessary to connect physically adjustable items, regular or liquid-tight flexible metal conduit can be used, but only in lengths not longer than 4 ft. Only devices that act on or sense the contained air, such as thermostats, are permitted. If lighting fixtures are installed for maintenance or repair, they must be of the enclosed gasketed type. This paragraph applies primarily to fabricated ducts and plenums.

(c) Other Space Used for Environmental Air. This paragraph applies to areas such as hung ceilings which are used for transporting air (return air or supply air plenums). Type MI cable and Type MC cable without an overall nonmetallic covering, as well as Type AC and other factory assembled multiconductor cable made to be installed in these areas may be used in these areas. Other types of cables and conductors can be used but only when installed in EMT, flexible metallic tubing, intermediate metal conduit, rigid metal conduit, wireways with metal covers or solid bottom metal cable tray with solid metal covers, or flexible metal conduit. Lighting fixtures and other electrical equipment can be installed in these areas if the unit is made for the ambient temperature. Also permitted is electric equipment with a metal enclosure or a listed nonmetallic enclosure with low smoke- and fire-resistive qualities unless prohibited in another place in the Code. There are five exceptions to the above:

1. Liquidtight flexible metal conduit can be used in lengths not longer than 6 ft.
2. When identified for this use, integral fan systems.
3. Habitable rooms or areas are not included as applicable spaces.
4. Prefabricated cable assemblies of metallic wiring systems without nonmetallic sheathing when approved for these areas.
5. Joist or stud spaces in dwelling units if wiring or equipment passes through perpendicular to long dimension.
6. Underfloor area in Section 645-2(c)(3).

(d) Data Processing Systems. Refer to Article 645.

B. Requirements for Over 600 Volts, Nominal

300-31 Covers Required

300-32 Conductors of Different Systems

Conductors of high- (over 600 V) and low-voltage systems cannot be in the same enclosure except in motors, switchgear, control assemblies, and the like, or in manholes with proper separation.

300-34 Conductor Bending Radius

300-35 Protection against Induction Heating

300-36 Grounding

ARTICLE 305
TEMPORARY WIRING

305-1 Scope

305-2 Other Articles

305-3 Time Constraints

305-4 General

305-5 Grounding

305-6 Ground—Fault Protection for Personnel

305-7 Guarding

ARTICLE 310
CONDUCTORS FOR GENERAL WIRING

310-1 Scope

Article 310 is to be used for general requirements for wiring, but not in areas where it is part of an integral device such as a motor, motor controller, or where covered in another part of the *NEC*®.

310-2 Conductors

Conductors must be insulated and made of copper, copper-clad aluminum, or aluminum unless otherwise specified in the *NEC*®.

310-3 Stranded Conductors

Any conductor installed in a raceway must be stranded if it is No. 8 or larger. This is not required if the conductor is used as a busbar, in Type MI cable, or as a bonding conductor described in Section 680-22(b).

310-4 Conductors in Parallel

Conductors 1/0 or larger can be run in parallel if they are the same length, the same size, and of the same material with the same insulation and terminated the same way. If run separately, the raceways must be the same. There are three exceptions to this:

1. Section 620-12(a)(1), Exception No. 2: elevator lighting.
2. If smaller than No. 1/0, used for control power to indicating instruments, relays, and similar devices, and in the same raceway, each individual conductor can carry the entire load and the overcurrent rating is not larger than the ampacity of any single conductor.
3. Sizes smaller than No. 1/0 are allowed for frequencies of 360 Hz and higher provided that Exception 2 is met.

310-5 Minimum Size of Conductors

Minimum sizes are shown in Table 310-5. For voltages up to 2000, it is No. 14 for copper and No. 12 for aluminum or copper-clad aluminum. The following exceptions apply:

1. Refer to Section 400-12 for flexible cords.
2. No. 18 may be used for fixture wire (Section 410-24).
3. Refer to Section 430-22 for fractional-horsepower motors.
4. Refer to Section 610-14 for cranes and hoists.
5. Refer to Section 620-12 for elevator control and signaling circuits.
6. Refer to Sections 725-16, 725-37, and 725-40 for Class 1, 2, and 3 circuits.
7. Refer to Sections 760-16, 760-27, and 760-30 for fire protective signaling circuits.
8. No. 14 copper and No. 12 aluminum or copper-clad aluminum can be used for Types AVA, AVB, and AVL cables rated 2001 to 5000 V.
9. When using Type V cable, exceptions are provided.

10. Refer to Section 430-72 for motor control circuits.

310-6 Shielding

310-7 Direct Burial Conductors

310-8 Wet Locations

Use only lead-covered conductors; Type RHW, TW, THW, THWN, or XHHW; or a type listed as such for a wet location.

310-9 Corrosive Conditions

310-10 Temperature Limitations of Conductors

310-11 Marking

All conductors and cables must have marked on them the rated voltage, the proper letter type, the manufacturer's name or trademark, and the size or circular mil area. The markings should be on the surface and spaced not more than 24 in. Certain cables can use marker tape inside the cable. Refer to this section in the *NEC*® for specific types where marker tape is permitted, which cables can have the size located elsewhere, and suffix designations for number of conductors.

310-12 Conductor Identification

(a) Grounded Conductors. Insulated grounded conductors generally must have an outer covering of white or natural gray. There are exceptions for multiconductor varnished-cloth-insulated cable, fixture wires, Type MI cable, requirements of Section 210-5(a), and where qualified persons only are used for maintenance and supervision as to where markings are permitted.

(b) Equipment Grounding Conductors. When insulated, they must generally have a cover of green or green with yellow stripes. There are exceptions for conductors larger than No. 6 and larger wires as to where the markings are permitted and the same exceptions for maintenance and supervision by qualified persons as to where the markings are permitted.

(c) **Ungrounded Conductors.** These may be any color except white, natural gray, or green.

310-13 Conductor Constructions and Applications

Insulated conductors must be in accordance with Tables 310-13 and 310-61 through 310-67.

310-14 Aluminum Conductor Material

310-15 Ampacity

The ratings for conductors of 0 to 2000 V are shown in Tables 310-16 through 310-31. For convenience only Tables 310-16 through 310-24 are shown here. The reader is referred to the Code for the additional tables, which are for cables in underground electric ducts, direct buried or multiconductor cable. A new definition for electrical duct is included. Additional tables for conductor application, insulation, and ampacities for voltages above 2000 V are noted in Tables 310-61 to 310-84. Since this section has been changed it is suggested that the reader become familiar with it in its entirety in the Code.

If more than one ampacity is determined from the tables or calculations, the lowest value must be used. If not included in the tables, the following formula can be used with engineering supervision:

$$I = \sqrt{\frac{TC - (TA + DELTA\ TD)}{RDC(1 + YC)RCA}}$$

TC = Conductor temperature in degrees C

TA = Ambient temperature in degrees C

DELTA TD = Dielectric loss temperature rise

RDC = DC resistance of conductor at temperature TC

YC = Component ac resistance resulting from skin effect and proximity effect

RCA = Effective thermal resistance between conductor and surrounding ambient

(FPN): The ampacities provided by this section are based on temperature alone and do not take voltage drop into consideration.

(FPN): Conductors of circuits as defined in Article 100, sized to prevent a voltage drop exceeding 5 percent, will provide reasonable efficiency of operation.

Notes to Tables 310-16 through 310-31 start on page 95.

ARTICLE 318
CABLE TRAYS

318-1 Scope

318-2 Definition

318-3 Uses Permitted

(a) Wiring Methods. The following types of cables can be used in cable trays provided they meet specific requirements found in the descriptions for each cable. The reader should refer to specific articles in the *NEC®* for additional requirements. The cables are:

1. Armored cable
2. Mineral-insulated, metal-sheathed cable
3. Power-limited tray cable
4. Metal-clad cable
5. Shielded nonmetallic-sheathed cable
6. Nonmetallic-sheathed cable
7. Multiconductor underground feeder and branch circuit conductor cable
8. Multiconductor service-entrance cable
9. Power and control tray cable
10. Other factory-assembled cable approved for this purpose
11. Approved conduit or raceway with its conductors

TABLE 310-16 Ampacities of Not More Than Three Single Insulated Conductors, Rated 0 through 2000 Volts, in Raceway in Free Air and Ampacities of Cable Types AC, NM, NMC and SE

Based on Ambient Air Temperature of 30°C (86°F)

Size	*Temperature Rating of Conductor. See Table 310-13.*								Size
	60°C (140°F)	*75°C (167°F)*	*85°C (185°F)*	*90°C (194°F)*	*60°C (140°F)*	*75°C (167°F)*	*85°C (185°F)*	*90°C (194°F)*	
AWG MCM	*Types †TW, †UF*	*Types †FEPW, †RH, †RHW, †THW, †THWN, †XHHW, †USE, †ZW*	*Type V*	*Types TA, TBS, SA, AVB, SIS, †FEP, †FEPB, †RHH, †THHN, †XHHW**	*Types †TW, †UF*	*Types †RH, †RHW, †THW, †THWN, †XHHW, †USE*	*Type V*	*Types TA, TBS, SA, AVB, SIS, †RHH, †THHN, †XHHW**	*AWG MCM*
	Copper				*Aluminum or Copper-Clad Aluminum*				
18	....	....	....	14	....	....	....	....	....
16	....	....	18	18	....	....	....	....	....
14	20†	20†	25	25†	....	....	....	....	....
12	25†	25†	30	30†	20†	20†	25	25†	12
10	30	35†	40	40†	25	30†	30	35†	10
8	40	50	55	55	30	40	40	45	8

6	55	65	70	75	40	50	55	60	6
4	70	85	95	95	55	65	75	75	4
3	85	100	110	110	65	75	85	85	3
2	95	115	125	130	75	90	100	100	2
1	110	130	145	150	85	100	110	115	1
1/0	125	150	165	170	100	120	130	135	1/0
2/0	145	175	190	195	115	135	145	150	2/0
3/0	165	200	215	225	130	155	170	175	3/0
4/0	195	230	250	260	150	180	195	205	4/0
250	215	255	275	290	170	205	220	230	250
300	240	285	310	320	190	230	250	255	300
350	260	310	340	350	210	250	270	280	350
400	280	335	365	380	225	270	295	305	400
500	320	380	415	430	260	310	335	350	500
600	355	420	460	475	285	340	370	385	600
700	385	460	500	520	310	375	405	420	700
750	400	475	515	535	320	385	420	435	750
800	410	490	535	555	330	395	430	450	800
900	435	520	565	585	355	425	465	480	900

TABLE 310-16 (continued)

Size	Temperature Rating of Conductor. See Table 310-13.								Size
	60°C (140°F)	75°C (167°F)	85°C (185°F)	90°C (194°F)	60°C (140°F)	75°C (167°F)	85°C (185°F)	90°C (194°F)	
AWG MCM	Types †TW, †UF	Types †FEPW, †RH, †RHW, †THW, †THWN, †XHHW, †USE, †ZW	Type V	Types TA, TBS, SA, AVB, SIS, †FEP, †FEPB, †RHH, †THHN, †XHHW*	Types †TW, †UF	Types †RH, †RHW, †THW, †THWN, †XHHW, †USE	Type V	Types TA, TBS, SA, AVB, SIS, †RHH, †THHN, †XHHW*	AWG MCM
	Copper				Aluminum or Copper-Clad Aluminum				
1000	455	545	590	615	375	445	485	500	1000
1250	495	590	640	665	405	485	525	545	1250
1500	520	625	680	705	435	520	565	585	1500
1750	545	650	705	735	455	545	595	615	1750
2000	560	665	725	750	470	560	610	630	2000

Ampacity Correction Factors

Ambient Temp. °C	For ambient temperatures other than 30°C (86°F), multiply the ampacities shown above by the appropriate factor shown below.								Ambient Temp. °F
21-25	1.08	1.05	1.04	1.04	1.08	1.05	1.04	1.04	70-77
26-30	1.00	1.00	1.00	1.00	1.00	1.00	1.00	1.00	79-86
31-35	.91	.94	.95	.96	.91	.94	.95	.96	88-95
36-40	.82	.88	.90	.91	.82	.88	.90	.91	97-104
41-45	.71	.82	.85	.87	.71	.82	.85	.87	106-113
46-50	.58	.75	.80	.82	.58	.75	.80	.82	115-122
51-55	.41	.67	.74	.76	.41	.67	.74	.76	124-131
56-60	....	.58	.67	.71	....	.58	.67	.71	133-140
61-70	....	.33	.52	.58	....	.33	.52	.58	142-158
71-80	....	....	.30	.41	....	....	.30	.41	160-176

† Unless otherwise specifically permitted elsewhere in this Code, the overcurrent protection for conductor types marked with an obelisk (†) shall not exceed 15 amperes for 14 AWG, 20 amperes for 12 AWG, and 30 amperes for 10 AWG copper; or 15 amperes for 12 AWG and 25 amperes for 10 AWG aluminum and copper-clad aluminum after any correction factors for ambient temperature and number of conductors have been applied.

* For dry and damp locations only. See 75°C column for wet locations.

TABLE 310-17 Ampacities of Single Insulated Conductors, Rated 0 through 2000 Volts, in Free Air

Based on Ambient Air Temperature of 30°C (86°F)

Size	*Temperature Rating of Conductor. See Table 310-13.*								*Size*
	60°C (140°F)	*75°C (167°F)*	*85°C (185°F)*	*90°C (194°F)*	*60°C (140°F)*	*75°C (167°F)*	*85°C (185°F)*	*90°C (194°F)*	
AWG MCM	*Type †TW*	*Types †FEPW, †RH, †RHW, †THW, †THWN, †XHHW, †ZW*	*Type V*	*Types TA, TBS, SA, AVB, SIS, †FEP, †FEPB, †RHH, †THHN, †XHHW*, MI*	*Type †TW*	*Types †RH, †RHW, †THW, †THWN, †XHHW*	*Type V*	*Types TA, TBS, SA, AVB, SIS, †RHH, †THHN, †XHHW*, MI*	*AWG MCM*
	Copper				*Aluminum or Copper-Clad Aluminum*				
18	....	....	....	18	....	....	....	....	....
16	....	....	23	24	....	....	....	....	....
14	25†	30†	30	35†	....	....	....	....	....
12	30†	35†	40	40†	25†	30†	30	35†	12
10	40†	50†	55	55†	35†	40†	40	40†	10
8	60	70	75	80	45	55	60	60	8

6	80	95	100	105	60	75	80	80	6
4	105	125	135	140	80	100	105	110	4
3	120	145	160	165	95	115	125	130	3
2	140	170	185	190	110	135	145	150	2
1	165	195	215	220	130	155	165	175	1
1/0	195	230	250	260	150	180	195	205	1/0
2/0	225	265	290	300	175	210	225	235	2/0
3/0	260	310	335	350	200	240	265	275	3/0
4/0	300	360	390	405	235	280	305	315	4/0
250	340	405	440	455	265	315	345	355	250
300	375	445	485	505	290	350	380	395	300
350	420	505	550	570	330	395	430	445	350
400	455	545	595	615	355	425	465	480	400
500	515	620	675	700	405	485	525	545	500
600	575	690	750	780	455	540	595	615	600
700	630	755	825	855	500	595	650	675	700
750	655	785	855	885	515	620	675	700	750
800	680	815	885	920	535	645	700	725	800
900	730	870	950	985	580	700	760	785	900

TABLE 310-17 (continued)

Size	*Temperature Rating of Conductor. See Table 310-13.*								*Size*
	60°C (140°F)	*75°C (167°F)*	*85°C (185°F)*	*90°C (194°F)*	*60°C (140°F)*	*75°C (167°F)*	*85°C (185°F)*	*90°C (194°F)*	
AWG MCM	*Type †TW*	*Types †FEPW, †RH, †RHW, †THW, †THWN, †XHHW, †ZW*	*Type V*	*Types TA, TBS, SA, AVB, SIS, †FEP, †FEPB, †RHH, †THHN, †XHHW*, MI*	*Type †TW*	*Types †RH, †RHW, †THW, †THWN, †XHHW*	*Type V*	*Types TA, TBS, SA, AVB, SIS, †RHH, †THHN, †XHHW*, MI*	*AWG MCM*
	Copper				*Aluminum or Copper-Clad Aluminum*				
1000	780	935	1020	1055	625	750	815	845	1000
1250	890	1065	1160	1200	710	855	930	960	1250
1500	980	1175	1275	1325	795	950	1035	1075	1500
1750	1070	1280	1395	1445	875	1050	1145	1185	1750
2000	1155	1385	1505	1560	960	1150	1250	1335	2000

Ampacity Correction Factors

Ambient Temp. °C	*For ambient temperatures other than 30°C (86°F), multiply the ampacities shown above by the appropriate factor shown below.*								*Ambient Temp. °F*
21-25	1.08	1.05	1.04	1.04	1.08	1.05	1.04	1.04	70-77
26-30	1.00	1.00	1.00	1.00	1.00	1.00	1.00	1.00	79-86
31-35	.91	.94	.95	.96	.91	.94	.95	.96	88-95
36-40	.82	.88	.90	.91	.82	.88	.90	.91	97-104
41-45	.71	.82	.85	.87	.71	.82	.85	.87	106-113
46-50	.58	.75	.80	.82	.58	.75	.80	.82	115-122
51-55	.41	.67	.74	.76	.41	.67	.74	.76	124-131
56-60	....	.58	.67	.71	....	.58	.67	.71	133-140
61-70	....	.33	.52	.58	....	.33	.52	.58	142-158
71-80	....	....	.30	.41	....	....	.30	.41	160-176

† Unless otherwise specifically permitted elsewhere in this Code, the overcurrent protection for conductor types marked with an obelisk (†) shall not exceed 15 amperes for 14 AWG, 20 amperes for 12 AWG, and 30 amperes for 10 AWG copper; or 15 amperes for 12 AWG and 25 amperes for 10 AWG aluminum and copper-clad aluminum.

* For dry and damp locations only. See 75°C column for wet locations.

TABLE 310-18 Ampacities of Three Single Insulated Conductors Rated 0 through 2000 Volts, 110° to 250°C, in Raceway in Free Air

Based on Ambient Air Temperature of 40°C (104°F)

Size	*Temperature Rating of Conductor. See Table 310-13.*									*Size*
	110°C (230°F)	*125°C (257°F)*	*150°C (302°F)*	*200°C (392°F)*	*250°C (482°F)*	*110°C (230°F)*	*125°C (257°F)*	*150°C (302°F)*	*200°C (392°F)*	
AWG MCM	*Types AVA, AVL*	*Types AI, AIA*	*Type Z*	*Types A, AA, FEP, FEPB, PFA*	*Types PFAH, TFE*	*Types AVA, AVL*	*Types AI, AIA*	*Type Z*	*Types A, AA*	*AWG MCM*
	Copper				*Nickel or Nickel-Coated Copper*	*Aluminum or Copper-Clad Aluminum*				
14	29	31	34	36	39	....	....	....	....	14
12	36	39	43	45	54	25	27	30	35	12
10	46	50	55	60	73	37	40	44	47	10
8	64	69	76	83	93	48	52	57	65	8

6	81	87	96	110	117	63	68	75	86	6
4	109	118	120	125	148	85	92	94	98	4
3	129	139	143	152	166	96	104	109	119	3
2	143	154	160	171	191	111	120	124	133	2
1	168	181	186	197	215	131	141	145	154	1
1/0	193	208	215	229	244	150	162	169	183	1/0
2/0	229	247	251	260	273	179	193	198	208	2/0
3/0	263	284	288	297	308	205	221	227	238	3/0
4/0	301	325	332	346	361	235	253	260	275	4/0
250	345	372	....	....	....	270	291	....	....	250
300	391	422	....	....	....	306	330	....	....	300
350	436	470	....	....	....	342	369	....	....	350
400	468	505	....	....	....	368	397	....	....	400
500	531	573	....	....	....	421	454	....	....	500
600	588	634	....	....	....	471	508	....	....	600
700	645	696	....	....	....	520	561	....	....	700
750	673	726	....	....	....	545	588	....	....	750
800	699	754	....	....	....	566	610	....	....	800
1000	785	846	....	....	....	651	701	....	....	1000
1500	961	....	....	....	....	795	....	....	....	1500
2000	1109	....	....	....	....	919	....	....	....	2000

TABLE 310-18 (continued)

Ampacity Correction Factors										
Ambient Temp. °C	*For ambient temperature other than 40°C (104°F), multiply the ampacities shown above by the appropriate factor shown below.*									*Ambient Temp. °F*
41-50	.93	.94	.95	.97	.98	.93	.94	.95	.97	106-122
51-60	.85	.87	.90	.94	.95	.85	.87	.90	.94	124-140
61-70	.76	.80	.85	.90	.93	.76	.80	.85	.90	142-158
71-80	.65	.73	.80	.87	.90	.65	.73	.80	.90	160-176
81-90	.53	.64	.74	.83	.87	.53	.64	.74	.83	177-194
91-100	.38	.54	.67	.79	.85	.38	.54	.67	.79	195-212
101-120	....	.24	.52	.71	.79	....	.24	.52	.71	213-248
121-140	....	....	.30	.61	.72	....	....	.30	.61	249-284
141-160	....	....	....	.50	.65	....	....	....	.50	285-320
161-180	....	....	....	.35	.58	....	....	....	.35	321-356
181-200	....	....	....	....	.49	....	....	....	....	357-392
201-225	....	....	....	....	.35	....	....	....	....	393-437

Notes to Tables 310-16 through 310-31*

1. Explanation of Tables

For explanation of Type Letters, and for recognized size of conductors for the various conductor insulations, see Section 310-13. For installation requirements, see Sections 310-1 through 310-10, and the various articles of this Code. For flexible cords, see Tables 400-4 and 400-5.

3. Three-Wire, Single-Phase Dwelling Services

In dwelling units, conductors, as listed below, shall be permitted to be utilized as three-wire, single-phase, service-entrance conductors and the three-wire, single-phase feeder that carries the total current supplied by that service. Grounded service-entrance conductors shall be permitted to be two AWG sizes smaller than the ungrounded conductors provided the requirements of Section 230-42 are met.

Conductor Types and Sizes
RH-RHH-RHW-THW-THWN-THHN-XHHW

Copper	*Aluminum and Copper-Clad AL*	*Service Rating in Amps*
AWG	AWG	
4	2	100
3	1	110
2	1/0	125
1	2/0	150
1/0	3/0	175
2/0	4/0	200

5. Bare Conductors

Where bare conductors are used with insulated conductors, their allowable ampacities shall be limited to that permitted for the adjacent insulated conductors.

* Notes continue on pages 99, 103, and 107.

TABLE 310-19 Ampacities for Single Insulated Conductors Rated 0 through 2000 Volts, 110° to 250°C, in Free Air

Based on Ambient Air Temperature of 40°C (104°F)

Size	*Temperature Rating of Conductor. See Table 310-13.*									*Size*
	110°C (230°F)	*125°C (257°F)*	*150°C (302°F)*	*200°C (392°F)*	*250°C (482°F)*	*110°C (230°F)*	*125°C (257°F)*	*150°C (302°F)*	*20°C (392°F)*	
AWG MCM	*Types AVA, AVL*	*Types AI, AIA*	*Type Z*	*Types A, AA, FEP, FEPB, PFA*	*Types PFAH, TFE*	*Types AVA, AVL*	*Types AI, AIA*	*Type Z*	*Types A, AA*	*AWG MCM*
	Copper				*Nickel or Nickel-Coated Copper*	*Aluminum or Copper-Clad Aluminum*				
14	39	42	46	54	59	....	....	....	....	14
12	51	55	60	68	78	40	43	47	54	12
10	67	72	80	90	107	53	57	63	71	10
8	90	97	106	124	142	70	75	83	96	8

6	121	131	155	165	205	95	102	112	128	6
4	160	172	190	220	278	125	135	148	171	4
3	180	194	214	252	327	144	155	170	196	3
2	215	232	255	293	381	167	180	198	227	2
1	247	266	293	344	440	193	208	228	267	1
1/0	286	309	339	399	532	222	239	263	310	1/0
2/0	329	355	390	467	591	257	277	305	363	2/0
3/0	380	410	451	546	708	296	319	351	443	3/0
4/0	446	481	529	629	830	347	374	411	490	4/0
250	493	532	....	....	....	384	414	....	....	250
300	552	595	....	....	....	431	464	....	....	300
350	611	659	....	....	....	477	514	....	....	350
400	663	715	....	....	....	518	559	....	....	400
500	767	827	....	....	....	600	647	....	....	500
600	860	928	....	....	....	674	727	....	....	600
700	953	1028	....	....	....	749	808	....	....	700
750	1000	1079	....	....	....	786	848	....	....	750
800	1039	1121	....	....	....	818	882	....	....	800
1000	1197	1291	....	....	....	947	1021	....	....	1000
1500	1465	1580	....	....	....	1160	1251	....	....	1500
2000	1692	1825	....	....	....	1340	1444	....	....	2000

TABLE 310-19 (continued)

Ampacity Correction Factors

Ambient Temp. °C	*For ambient temperature other than 40°C (104°F), multiply the ampacities shown above by the appropriate factor shown below.*									*Ambient Temp. °F*
41-50	.93	.94	.95	.97	.98	.93	.94	.95	.97	106-122
51-60	.85	.87	.90	.94	.95	.85	.87	.90	.94	124-140
61-70	.76	.80	.85	.90	.93	.76	.80	.85	.90	142-158
71-80	.65	.73	.80	.87	.90	.65	.73	.80	.87	160-176
81-90	.53	.64	.74	.83	.87	.53	.64	.74	.83	177-194
91-100	.38	.54	.67	.79	.85	.38	.54	.67	.79	195-212
101-120	....	.24	.52	.71	.79	....	.24	.52	.71	213-248
121-140	....	....	.30	.61	.72	....	....	.30	.61	249-284
141-160	....	....	....	.50	.65	....	....	....	.50	285-320
161-180	....	....	....	.35	.58	....	....	....	.35	321-356
181-200	....	....	....	....	.49	....	....	....	....	357-392
201-225	....	....	....	....	.35	....	....	....	....	393-437

6. Mineral-Insulated, Metal-Sheathed Cable

The temperature limitation on which the ampacities of mineral-insulated, metal-sheathed cable are based is determined by the insulating materials used in the end seal. Termination fittings incorporating unimpregnated, organic, insulating materials are limited to 90°C operation.

7. Type MTW Machine Tool Wire

(FPN): For the ampacities of Type MTW wire, see Table 13-1(c) in the Electrical Standard for Industrial Machinery (NFPA 79-1985).

8. Ampacity Adjustment Factors

(a) More Than Three Conductors in a Raceway or Cable. Where the number of conductors in a raceway or cable exceeds three, the ampacities given in Tables 310-16 or 310-18, 310-22, 310-26, 310-27, 310-28, 310-29, 310-30, and 310-31 shall be reduced as shown in the following table:

Number of Conductors	*Percent of Values in Tables 310-16, 310-18, 310-22, 310-26, 310-27, 310-28, 310-29, 310-30, and 310-31, as Adjusted for Ambient Temperature if Necessary*
4 thru 6	80
7 thru 9	70
10 thru 24*	70
25 thru 42*	60
43 and above*	50

* These factors include the effects of a load diversity of 50 percent.

Where single conductors or multiconductor cables are stacked or bundled longer than 24 inches (610 mm) without maintaining spacing and are not

TABLE 310-22 Ampacities of Three Insulated Conductors, Rated 0 through 2000 Volts, Within an Overall Covering (Three Conductor Cable), in Raceway in Free Air

Based on Ambient Air Temperature of 30°C (86°F)

Size	*Temperature Rating of Conductor. See Table 310-13.*						*Size*
	60°C (140°F)	*75°C (167°F)*	*90°C (194°F)*	*60°C (140°F)*	*75°C (167°F)*	*90°C (194°F)*	
AWG MCM	*Type †TW*	*Types †RH, †RHW, †THW, †THWN, †XHHW*, †ZW*	*Types †THHN, †RHH, †XHHW**	*Type †TW*	*Types †RH, †RHW, †THW, †THWN, †XHHW*	*Types †THHN, †RHH, †XHHW**	*AWG MCM*
	Copper			*Aluminum or Copper-Clad Aluminum*			
14	16†	18†	21†	....	....	....	14
12	20†	24†	27†	16†	18†	21†	12
10	27†	33†	36†	21†	25†	28†	10
8	36	43	48	28	33	37	8

6	48	58	65	38	45	51	6
4	66	79	89	51	61	69	4
3	76	90	102	59	70	79	3
2	88	105	119	69	83	93	2
1	102	121	137	80	95	106	1
1/0	121	145	163	94	113	127	1/0
2/0	138	166	186	108	129	146	2/0
3/0	158	189	214	124	147	167	3/0
4/0	187	223	253	147	176	197	4/0
250	205	245	276	160	192	217	250
300	234	281	317	185	221	250	300
350	255	305	345	202	242	273	350
400	274	328	371	218	261	295	400
500	315	378	427	254	303	342	500
600	343	413	468	279	335	378	600
700	376	452	514	310	371	420	700
750	387	466	529	321	384	435	750
800	397	479	543	331	397	450	800
900	415	500	570	350	421	477	900
1000	448	542	617	382	460	521	1000

TABLE 310-22 (continued)

Ambient Temp. °C	*For ambient temperatures other than 30°C (86°F) multiply the ampacities shown above by the appropriate factor shown below.*						Ambient Temp. °F
21-25	1.08	1.05	1.04	1.08	1.05	1.04	70-77
26-30	1.00	1.00	1.00	1.00	1.00	1.00	79-86
31-35	.91	.94	.96	.91	.94	.96	88-95
36-40	.82	.88	.91	.82	.88	.91	97-104
41-45	.71	.82	.87	.71	.82	.87	106-113
46-50	.58	.75	.82	.58	.75	.82	115-122
51-55	.41	.67	.76	.41	.67	.76	124-131
56-60	....	.58	.71	....	.58	.71	133-140
61-70	....	.33	.58	....	.33	.58	142-158
71-80	....	....	.41	....	....	.41	160-176

† Unless otherwise specifically permitted elsewhere in this Code, the overcurrent protection for conductor types marked with an obelisk (†) shall not exceed 15 amperes for 14 AWG, 20 amperes for 12 AWG, and 30 amperes for 10 AWG copper; or 15 amperes for 12 AWG and 25 amperes for 10 AWG aluminum and copper-clad aluminum.

* For dry and damp locations only. See 75°C column for wet locations.

installed in raceways, the ampacity of each conductor shall be reduced as shown in the above table.

Exception No. 1: When conductors of different systems, as provided in Section 300-3, are installed in a common raceway the derating factors shown above shall apply to the number of power and lighting (Articles 210, 215, 220, and 230) conductors only.

Exception No. 2: For conductors installed in cable trays, the provisions of Section 318-11 shall apply.

Exception No. 3: Derating factors do not apply to conductors in nipples having a length not exceeding 24 inches (610 mm).

Exception No. 4: Derating factors do not apply to underground conductors entering or leaving an outdoor trench if those conductors have physical protection in the form of rigid metal conduit, intermediate metal conduit or rigid nonmetallic conduit Schedule 80 having a length not exceeding 10 feet (3.05 m) and the number of conductors in a conduit does not exceed 4.

(b) More Than One Conduit, Tube, or Raceway. Spacing between conduits, tubing, or raceways shall be maintained.

9. Overcurrent Protection

Where the standard ratings and settings of overcurrent devices do not correspond with the ratings and settings allowed for conductors, the next higher standard rating and setting shall be permitted.

Exception: As limited in Section 240-3.

10. Neutral Conductor

(a) A neutral conductor which carries only the unbalanced current from other conductors, as in the case of normally balanced circuits of three or more conductors, shall not be counted when applying the provisions of Note 8.

TABLE 310-23 Ampacities of Two or Three Single Insulated Conductors, Rated 0 through 2000 Volts, Supported on a Messenger

Based on Ambient Air Temperature of 40°C (104°F)

Size	*Temperature Rating of Conductor. See Table 310-13.*				*Size*
	75°C (167°F)	*90°C (194°F)*	*75°C (167°F)*	*90°C (194°F)*	
AWG MCM	*Types RH, RHW, THW, THWN, XHHW, ZW*	*Types THHN, RHH, XHHW**	*Types RH, RHW, THW, THWN, XHHW*	*Types THHN, RHH, XHHW**	*AWG MCM*
	Copper		*Aluminum or Copper-Clad Aluminum*		
8	57	66	44	51	8
6	76	89	59	69	6
4	101	117	78	91	4
3	118	138	92	107	3
2	135	158	106	123	2
1	158	185	123	144	1

1/0	183	214	143	167	1/0
2/0	212	247	165	193	2/0
3/0	245	287	192	224	3/0
4/0	287	335	224	262	4/0
250	320	374	251	292	250
300	359	419	282	328	300
350	397	464	312	364	350
400	430	503	339	395	400
500	496	580	392	458	500
600	553	647	440	514	600
700	610	714	488	570	700
750	638	747	512	598	750
800	660	773	532	622	800
900	704	826	572	669	900
1000	748	879	612	716	1000

TABLE 310-23 (continued)

Ambient Temp. °C	*For ambient temperatures other than 40°C (104°F) multiply the ampacities shown above by the appropriate factor shown below.*				*Ambient Temp. °F*
21-25	1.20	1.14	1.20	1.14	70-77
26-30	1.13	1.10	1.13	1.10	79-86
31-35	1.07	1.05	1.07	1.05	88-95
36-40	1.00	1.00	1.00	1.00	97-104
41-45	.93	.95	.93	.95	106-113
46-50	.85	.89	.85	.89	119-122
51-55	.76	.84	.76	.84	124-131
56-60	.65	.77	.65	.77	133-140
61-70	.38	.63	.38	.63	142-158
71-80	....	.45	....	.45	160-176

* For dry and damp locations only. See 75°C column for wet locations.

(b) In a 3-wire circuit consisting of 2-phase wires and the neutral of a 4-wire, 3-phase wye-connected system, a common conductor carries approximately the same current as the other conductors and shall be counted when applying the provisions of Note 8.

(c) On a 4-wire, 3-phase wye circuit where the major portion of the load consists of electric-discharge lighting, data processing, or similar equipment, there are harmonic currents present in the neutral conductor and the neutral shall be considered to be a current-carrying conductor.

11. Grounding or Bonding Conductor

A grounding or bonding conductor shall not be counted when applying the provisions of Note 8.

(continued from pg. 83)

(b) In industrial establishments with only qualified maintenance personnel, additional types of cables or conductors with certain restrictions are permitted, including a single conductor 250 MCM or larger, and the conductor must be approved for cable tray use. The trays must be ladder, ventilated, 4-in.-ventilated channel, or 6-in. ventilated channel type, and multiconductor cable must be type MV. In all cases the cable must be sunlight resistant if exposed to the sun.

318-4 Uses Not Permitted

Cable trays cannot be used where they are exposed to severe physical injury and in hoistways.

318-5 Construction Specifications

Cable trays must have proper strength and rigidity, smooth edges, be protected against corrosion, have side rails, and contain the proper fittings. Flame-retardant material must be used for nonmetallic cable tray.

TABLE 310-24 Ampacities for Bare or Covered Conductors Based on 40°C Ambient, 80°C Total Conductor Temperature, 2 Feet (610 mm) per Second Wind Velocity

Bare Copper Conductors		*Covered Copper Conductors*		*Bare AAC Aluminum Conductor*		*Covered AAC Aluminum*	
AWG MCM	*AMPS*	*AWG MCM*	*AMPS*	*AWG MCM*	*AMPS*	*AWG MCM*	*AMPS*
8	98	8	103	8	76	8	80
6	124	6	130	6	96	6	101
4	155	4	163	4	121	4	127
2	209	2	219	2	163	2	171
1/0	282	1/0	297	1/0	220	1/0	231
2/0	329	2/0	344	2/0	255	2/0	268
3/0	382	3/0	401	3/0	297	3/0	312
4/0	444	4/0	466	4/0	346	4/0	364
250	494	250	519	266.8	403	266.8	423
300	556	300	584	336.4	468	336.4	492
500	773	500	812	397.5	522	397.5	548
750	1000	750	1050	477.0	588	477.0	617
1000	1193	1000	1253				

		556.5	650	556.5	682
		636.0	709	636.0	744
		795.0	819	795.0	860
		954.0	920		
		1033.5	968	1033.5	1017
		1272	1103	1272	1201
		1590	1267	1590	1381
		2000	1454	2000	1527

318-6 Installation

The cable tray system must be installed completely as a system before the cables are installed, have the proper supports, and have covers where required. Multiconductor cables can be installed in the same tray if 600 V or less. Cables over 600 V cannot be installed with cables under 600 V, with two exceptions. The cable trays must be exposed and accessible and have room around them for adequate access. They can go through partitions, walls, and floors if installed in accordance with Section 300-21 (proper and approved firestopping methods used).

318-7 Grounding

Proper grounding must be attained in compliance with Article 250. The entire system must be grounded. Minimum size steel and aluminum trays are indicated in Table 318-6(b)(2) of the *NEC®*.

318-8 Cable Installation

(a) Splices are permitted if approved methods are used, they are accessible, and are not over the side rails.

(b) Cables must be fastened in sloping or vertical runs.

(c) If the cable is installed in a bushed conduit for protection, a box is not required.

(d) If installed in parallel, the conductors must be grouped with one conductor per phase in each group. Single conductors must be bound to circuit groups.

318-9 Number of Multiconductor Cables, Rated 2000 Volts, Nominal, or Less, in Cable Trays

Refer to this section in the Code and Table 318-9.

318-10 Number of Single Conductor Cables, Rated 2000 Volts or Less, in Cable Trays

Refer to this section in the Code and Table 318-10.

318-11 Ampacity of Cables Rated 2000 Volts or Less in Cable Trays

Do not use the derating factors of Note 8 to Tables 310-16 through 310-31.

(a) Multiconductor Cables. Multiconductor cables, rated 2000 V or less, installed as per Section 318-9 are to follow ampacities in Tables 310-18 and 310-21. If the tray is covered for more than 6 ft with a solid unventilated cover, the ampacities allowed are 95% of those shown in the tables. An additional exception is allowed for in a layer of uncovered trays.

(b) Single Conductor Cables. Single conductor or single conductors cabled together, rated 2000 V or less, properly installed in accordance with the Code, are to use ampacities as follows:

1. Cables 600 MCM and larger in uncovered trays use not more than 75% of the ampacities in Tables 310-17 and 310-19. If the tray is covered for more than 6 ft with unventilated covers, use a maximum 70% of the ampacities in the tables.
2. Cables 250 MCM through 500 MCM in uncovered trays use not more than 65% of the ampacities in Tables 310-17 and 310-19. If the tray is covered for more than 6 ft with unventilated covers, use a maximum 60% of the ampacities in the tables.
3. If single conductor cables are placed in a single layer with at least one cable diameter

separation, the tray is uncovered and the cable is 250 MCM or larger, the ampacities in Tables 310-17 and 310-19 may be used.

4. Special allowance when installed in uncovered tray with a triangular configuration.

318-12 Number of Type MV and MC Cables (2001 Volts or Over) in Cable Trays

318-13 Ampacity of Type MV and Type MC Cables (2001 Volts or Over) in Cable Trays

ARTICLE 320
OPEN WIRING ON INSULATORS

320-1 Definition

This type of wiring is exposed with a single insulated conductor using an insulator (knob, cleat, tube, or flexible tubing) for protection and support.

320-2 Other Articles

Must also comply with Articles 225 and 320 as well as other Code articles that apply.

320-3 Uses Permitted

This type of wiring can be used only where the nominal voltage does not exceed 600 V, in industrial or agricultural structures, both indoors or outdoors, both wet or dry locations, for services, and where corrosive vapors are present.

320-5 Conductors

320-6 Conductor Supports

320-7 Mounting of Conductor Supports

320-8 Tie Wires

320-10 Flexible Nonmetallic Tubing

320-11 Through Walls, Floors, Wood Cross Members, etc.

320-12 Clearance from Piping, Exposed Conductors, etc.

320-13 Entering Spaces Subject to Dampness, Wetness, or Corrosive Vapors

320-14 Protection from Physical Damage

320-15 Unfinished Attics and Roof Spaces

320-16 Switches

ARTICLE 321
MESSENGER-SUPPORTED WIRE

321-1 Definition

This type of wiring is exposed using a messenger wire as a support for insulated conductors. These conductors are usually in the form of a type of cable. In some instances in industrial establishments, insulated wire can be used as well as cable.

321-2 Other Articles

Must also comply with Articles 225 and 300 as well as other Code articles that apply.

321-3 Uses Permitted

321-4 Uses Not Permitted

321-5 Ampacity

321-6 Messenger Support

321-7 Grounding

321-8 Conductor Splices and Taps

ARTICLE 324
CONCEALED KNOB-AND-TUBE WIRING

324-1 Definition

This type of wiring is concealed in hollow spaces in buildings (walls and ceilings) with a single insulated conductor using knobs, tubes, and flexible nonmetallic tubing for support and protection.

324-2 Other Articles

It must also comply with Article 300 as well as other Code articles that apply.

324-3 Uses Permitted

It can only be used to extend an existing installation with special permission from the authorities having jurisdiction and only in hollow spaces of walls and ceilings and unfinished attic and roof spaces (refer to Section 324-11 in the *NEC*®).

324-4 Uses Not Permitted

It is not allowed in commercial garages, motion picture studios, classified hazardous locations, and theaters and similar locations, or in hollow spaces of walls, ceilings, and attics under certain conditions.

324-5 Conductors

324-6 Conductor Supports

324-7 Tie Wires

324-8 Conductor Clearances

324-9 Through Walls, Floors, Wood Cross Members, etc.

324-10 Clearance from Piping, Exposed Conductors, etc.

324-11 Unfinished Attics and Roof Spaces

324-12 Splices

324-13 Boxes

324-14 Switches

ARTICLE 325
INTEGRATED GAS SPACER CABLE
Type IGS

A. General

325-1 Definition

325-2 Other Articles

325-3 Uses Permitted

325-4 Uses Not Permitted

B. Installation

325-11 Bending Radius

325-12 Bends

325-13 Fittings

325-14 Ampacity

C. Construction Specifications

325-20 Conductors

325-21 Insulation

325-22 Conduit

325-23 Grounding

325-24 Marking

ARTICLE 326
MEDIUM VOLTAGE CABLE
Type MV

326-1 Definition

This cable is rated above 2000 V and is a single or multiconductor solid dielectric insulated cable.

326-2 Other Articles

It must also comply with Articles 300, 305, 310, 318, 501, and 710 as well as other Code articles that apply.

326-3 Uses Permitted

It can be used in dry or wet locations, in raceways, directly buried, and in messenger-supported cable in systems up to 35,000 V. Refer to Sections 318-3(b) and 710-3(b).

326-4 Uses Not Permitted

It cannot be used in cable trays or direct sunlight unless approved for those purposes.

326-5 Construction

326-6 Ampacity

326-7 Markings

ARTICLE 328
FLAT CONDUCTOR CABLE
Type FCC

328-1 Scope

The wiring covered in this article is a field-installed system to be used for branch circuits under carpet squares.

328-2 Definitions

The reader is referred to the Code for these definitions.

328-3 Other Articles

It must also comply with Articles 210, 220, 240, 250, and 300 as well as other Code articles that apply.

328-4 Uses Permitted

It can be used for general-purpose, appliance, and individual branch circuits; on floors that are hard, sound, or smooth made of materials like or similar to concrete, ceramic, composition, and wood; on walls in surface metal raceways; in damp locations; and on floors where the temperature is higher than 86°F if approved for those temperatures.

328-5 Uses Not Permitted

It cannot be used outdoors, in wet locations, in classified hazardous locations, where there is corrosive vapor present, or in residential, school, or hospital buildings.

328-6 Branch-Circuit Ratings

The voltage ratings are up to 150 V to ground and up to 300 V between ungrounded conductors. The current ratings are up to 20 A for general-purpose and appliance branch circuits and up to 30 A for individual branch circuits.

B. Installation

328-10 Coverings

When on a floor, it must be covered with carpet squares. Release-type adhesive only is permitted.

328-11 Cable Connections and Insulating Ends

328-12 Shields

328-13 Enclosure and Shield Connections

328-14 Receptacles

They must be approved for this system.

328-15 Connection to Other Systems

Use approved transition assemblies.

328-16 Anchoring

328-17 Crossings

328-18 System Height

If it exceeds 0.09 in. it must be feathered or tapered at the edges to floor level.

328-19 FCC Systems Alterations

328-20 Polarization of Connections

C. Construction

328-30 Type FCC Cable

Three, four, or five flat copper conductors; one is an equipment grounding conductor.

328-31 Markings

328-32 Conductor Identification

328-33 Corrosion Resistance

328-34 Insulation

328-35 Shields

328-36 Receptacles and Housings

328-37 Transition Assemblies

ARTICLE 330 MINERAL-INSULATED, METAL-SHEATHED CABLE Type MI

A. General

330-1 Definition

Type MI cable is factory assembled with one or more conductors using a highly compressed refractory mineral insulation. The entire assembly is covered with a gastight and liquidtight copper sheath.

330-2 Other Articles

It must also comply with Article 300 as well as other Code articles that apply.

330-3 Uses Permitted

It can be used for services, feeders, and branch circuits; wet or dry locations; exposed or concealed; indoors or outdoors; embedded in concrete, plaster, fill, and other masonry; hazardous locations; underground when protected; corrosive locations that will not harm the sheath; and where exposed to gasoline and oil.

330-4 Uses Not Permitted

Where exposed to corrosive materials that will harm the sheath unless it is properly protected.

B. Installation

330-10 Wet Locations

330-11 Through Joists, Studs or Rafters

330-12 Supports

330-13 Bends

330-14 Fittings

330-15 Terminal Seals

C. Construction Specifications

330-20 Conductors

Solid copper.

330-21 Insulation

Highly compressed refractor mineral.

330-22 Outer Sheath

Copper that ensures mechanical protection, ground path, and a moisture seal.

ARTICLE 331
ELECTRICAL NONMETALLIC TUBING

A. General

331-1 Definition

331-2 Other Articles

331-3 Uses Permitted

331-4 Uses Not Permitted

B. Installation

331-5 Size

331-6 Number of Conductors in Tubing

331-7 Trimming

331-8 Joints

331-9 Bends—How Made

331-10 Bends—Number in One Run

331-11 Supports

331-12 Boxes and Fittings

331-13 Splices and Taps

331-14 Bushings

C. Construction Specifications

331-15 General

ARTICLE 333
ARMORED CABLE
Type AC

333-1 Definition

This type of cable is composed of insulated conductors in a flexible metal enclosure.

333-2 Other Articles

It must also comply with Article 300 as well as other Code articles that apply.

333-3 Marking

333-4 Construction

The cable consists of insulated conductors enclosed in a flexible metal armor with a copper or aluminum bonding strip inside and in contact with the armor (bonding strip not required for Type ACL).

333-5 Conductors

333-6 Use

It can be used for branch circuits or feeders, both concealed and exposed. Type AC can be used only in dry locations; Type ACL (lead-covered conductors) is to be used when there is a lot of moisture or dampness. It can also be used in plaster finish on brick or other masonry. This type of cable cannot be used in theaters, motion picture studios, hazardous locations, where there are corrosive vapors or fumes, cranes or hoists, storage battery rooms, in hoistways or on elevators in commercial garages, or elsewhere when prohibited by the *NEC*®. Refer to sections on individual locations for specific exceptions or restrictions.

333-7 Supports

333-8 Bends

333-9 Boxes and Fittings

333-10 Through Studs, Joists and Rafters

333-11 Exposed Work

333-12 In Accessible Attics

ARTICLE 334
METAL-CLAD CABLE

A. General

334-1 Definition

Metal-clad cable is Type MC. It is a cable in which the conductors are enclosed in a metal sheath, insulated, and the entire cable is put together at the factory.

334-2 Other Articles

This type of cable must be in accordance with Article 300 as well as other Code articles that apply.

334-3 Uses Permitted

This cable can be used for almost all types of applications, including wet locations, provided that it will not sustain physical damage and is not prohibited in another part of the *NEC®*. In wet locations one of the following must be adhered to: moisture will not get through the metal cover, a lead sheath that will not let moisture through is put under the metal cover, or the insulated conductors enclosed by the metal cover are approved for a wet location.

334-4 Uses Not Permitted

This cable cannot be used in a location where it is subject to corrosive conditions that are destructive. The *NEC®* gives as examples direct buried cable in earth or concrete, under fills, chlorides, caustic alkalis, and the like. If the metal cover will withstand these reactions, it can be used in such locations.

B. Installation

334-10 Installation

When installed in cable tray, direct buried, as service-entrance cable outside buildings, or as aerial cable, you must refer to the appropriate articles in the *NEC*®. It must be held at least every 6 ft.

334-11 Bending Radius

The following are the allowable radii of the curve of the inner edge: for shielded conductors, use the greater of either 12 times the diameter of one conductor or 7 times the overall diameter of the cable; for interlocked armor or corrugated sheath, 7 times the diameter of the sheath; for smooth sheath, use the following:

Cable up to ¾ in. diameter: 10 times diameter
Cable between ¾ and 1½ in. diameter: 12 times diameter
Cable larger than 1½ in. diameter: 15 times diameter

334-12 Fittings

334-13 Ampacity

You must use the ampacities in accordance with Section 310-15 with the exception of cable tray.

Cable tray: Sections 318-11 and 318-13.

C. Construction Specifications

334-20 Conductors

Copper, aluminum, or copper-clad aluminum must be used, either stranded or solid. The smallest sizes allowed are No. 18 for copper and No. 12 for aluminum or copper-clad aluminum.

334-21 Insulation

334-22 Metallic Sheath

The sheath must be either smooth, welded, and corrugated or interlocking.

334-23 Grounding

334-24 Marking

ARTICLE 336
NONMETALLIC-SHEATHED CABLE
Types NM and NMC

A. General

336-1 Definition

Nonmetallic-sheathed cable is either Type NM or NMC. It is a cable in which the insulated cables are enclosed in a nonmetallic material that is moisture-resistant and flame-retardant. The cable is put together at the factory.

336-2 Other Articles

Note other applicable articles, such as Article 300 and Article 316.

336-3 Uses Permitted

This type of cable can be used only in buildings that do not exceed three floors above grade. Type NM cable can be used either exposed or concealed in dry locations. It can be used in the voids of masonry or tile if not a damp location. Type NMC cable can be used where type NM cable is used and also in moist damp and corrosive areas and in walls of masonry block and the like.

336-4 Uses Not Permitted

Type NM or NMC cannot be used as service-entrance cable, in commercial garages, in motion picture studios, in theaters, and the like unless otherwise provided in the *NEC*®, in hoistways, storage battery rooms, hazardous locations, and in poured concrete cement or aggregate. The reader is referred to this section of the *NEC*® for a complete list of locations where types NM and NMC are not permitted.

B. Installation

336-10 Exposed Work

336-11 Through Studs, Joists and Rafters

336-12 In Unfinished Basements

336-13 In Accessible Attics

336-14 Bends

336-15 Supports

The cable must be secured at least every 4½ ft and not more than 12 in. from a fitting, box, or cabinet. Two exceptions noted are for a device that has an integral clamp and in prefabricated buildings.

336-16 Devices of Insulating Material

336-17 Boxes of Insulating Material

336-18 Devices with Integral Enclosures

C. Construction

336-25 Construction

The minimum size wire to be used is No. 14 for copper conductors and No. 12 for aluminum or copper-clad aluminum. In either case the maximum size is No. 2.

336-26 Conductors

The conductors to be used must be listed in Table 310-13 for use in branch circuits or in this type of cable. The conductors must be rated at 90°C (194°F). The ampacity to be used is listed in Table 310-15 under 60°C (140°F).

336-27 Marking

ARTICLE 337
SHIELDED NONMETALLIC-SHEATHED CABLE
Type SNM

337-1 Definition

This cable is Type SNM. It is factory assembled and has insulated conductors. It is placed in an extruded core of a flame-resistant, moisture-retardant material. It is covered with metal tape and wire shield. The entire assembly is jacketed with an extruded nonmetallic material that is moisture-, flame-, oil-, corrosion-, fungus-, and sunlight-resistant.

337-2 Other Articles

Conform to other Code articles where applicable.

337-3 Uses Permitted

It can only be used in cable trays or raceways, and in hazardous locations, when permitted, where the operating temperatures are not more than those of the cable.

337-4 Bends

337-5 Handling

337-6 Fittings

337-7 Bonding

The wire shield must be bonded to the ground bus and the ground bus at the supply point.

337-8 Construction

The conductors can be Type TFN, TFFN, THHN, or THWN maximum size No. 2 and minimum No. 18 for copper and No. 12 for aluminum or copper-clad aluminum.

337-9 Marking

ARTICLE 338
SERVICE-ENTRANCE CABLE
Types SE and USE

338-1 Definition

This cable is either Type SE or USE and is used primarily for services. Type SE has a flame-retardant and moisture-resistant cover. Type USE, which is the one used underground, has a moisture-resistant cover.

338-2 Uses Permitted as Service-Entrance Conductors

When used as service-entrance conductors, you must follow Article 230.

338-3 Uses Permitted as Branch Circuits or Feeders

(a) Grounded Conductor Insulated. Type SE can be used if all conductors are rubber-covered or thermoplastic type.

(b) Grounded Conductor Not Insulated. Generally, Type SE Cable with a noninsulated grounded conductor cannot be used for branch circuit or feeder wiring in a building. There are exceptions with specific rules for ranges, wall-mounted ovens, counter-mounted cooking units, or clothes dryers.

(c) Temperature Limitations. Do not exceed temperature specified.

338-4 Installation Methods

Review applicable sections of the *NEC®*.

338-5 Marking

ARTICLE 339
UNDERGROUND FEEDER AND BRANCH-CIRCUIT CABLE
Type UF

339-1 Description and Marking

This cable is Type UF. Sizes allowed are Minimum No. 14 copper or No. 12 aluminum or copper-clad aluminum and maximum No. 4/0. The conductors must be of the moisture-resistant type found in Table 310-13. It must be suitable for branch-circuit wiring and the ampacity to use is listed under 60°C (140°F) in Table 310-16. The overall covering must be flame-retardant, moisture-, fungus-, and corrosion-resistant, and able to be directly buried.

339-2 Other Articles

Conform to other Code articles where applicable, in particular Article 300 and Section 310-13.

339-3 Use

(a) Uses Permitted. In underground, including direct burial, as a feeder or branch circuit as long as the overcurrent requirements of Section 240-3 are adhered to. It can be used for interior wiring in wet, dry, or corrosive areas provided that all other conditions are met. In certain of these cases, as described in Section 690-31, it can not be used for solar photovoltaic systems.

(b) Uses Not Permitted. This type of cable cannot be used for service entrances, in commercial garages, in theaters, in storage battery rooms, in motion picture studios, in hazardous locations, in hoistways, in poured cement, or where exposed to direct rays of sun unless approved for sunlight installation.

339-4 Overcurrent Protection

339-5 Rated Ampacity

ARTICLE 340
POWER AND CONTROL TRAY CABLE
Type TC

340-1 Definition

This cable is Type TC. It is nonmetallic-sheathed cable approved for use in cable trays, raceways, or supported by messenger wire with insulated conductors. The grounding conductor can be either bare or covered.

340-2 Other Articles

Conform to other Code articles where applicable, in particular Articles 300 and 318.

340-3 Construction

Minimum-size conductors are No. 18 for copper and No. 12 for aluminum and copper-clad aluminum. Maximum size is 1000 MCM. Conductors of No. 18 and No. 16 sizes are to be in accordance with Section 725-16. All others are to be of the types shown in Table 310-13 or 310-62. The sheath is to be flame-retardant and nonmetallic. A metallic sheath cannot be put over or under the nonmetallic sheath. If it is installed in a wet area, it must also be moisture- and corrosion-resistant as applicable.

340-4 Uses Permitted

This cable can be used for power, lighting, control, signal and communications circuits; in cable trays, raceways, or supported by messenger wire; in hazardous locations when permitted in Articles 318 and 501; and where permitted by Article 725 for Class I circuits.

340-5 Uses Not Permitted

Type TC cable cannot be used where exposed to physical damage; on open brackets; where exposed to direct sunlight unless sunlight resistant; and direct buried unless approved for that purpose.

340-6 Marking

340-7 Ampacity

Use Table 400-5 and Section 318-11.

ARTICLE 342
NONMETALLIC EXTENSIONS

342-1 Definition

This is a conductor arrangement with two insulated conductors in a nonmetallic jacket or thermoplastic cover.

342-2 Other Articles

342-3 Uses Permitted

Only from an existing 15- or 20-A outlet on a branch circuit. It must be run exposed and dry. For surface extensions the buildings must only be occupied for residential or office use and with height restrictions of Section 336-3.

342-4 Uses Not Permitted

This type of extension cannot be used as an aerial cable other than where permitted; in unfinished areas, where there are corrosive vapors, through a floor or partition; and where the voltage between conductors is greater than 150 V for surface work and 300 V for aerial cable.

342-5 Splices and Taps

342-6 Fittings

342-7 Installation

342-8 Marking

ARTICLE 344
UNDERPLASTER EXTENSIONS

344-1 Use

This type of extension can be used only in a fire-resistant building on an existing branch circuit.

344-2 Materials

Use only rigid or flexible metal conduit; Type AC cable; intermediate metal conduit, rigid nonmetallic conduit; MI cable, electrical metallic tubing, MC cable, electrical nonmetallic tubing, or metal raceways.

344-3 Boxes and Fittings

344-4 Installation

It can be used on the face of masonry or other material and buried in the plaster finish.

344-5 Extension to Another Floor

It is not permitted unless in an approved raceway or cable.

ARTICLE 345
INTERMEDIATE METAL CONDUIT

A. General

345-1 Definition

This conduit is a circular metal raceway with all its couplings, etc.

345-2 Other Articles

Must be in accordance with Article 300.

345-3 Uses Permitted

Intermediate metal conduit can be used in most places and under most conditions. With the exception of aluminum fittings and enclosures and steel conduit, dissimilar metals in contact must not be used where possible. It can be used in the earth or in corrosive locations if it has corrosion protection. It can be used in cinder fill only if 2 in. of noncinder concrete is in direct contact, the conduit is 18 in. or more under the fill, or there is proper corrosion protection.

B. Installation

345-5 Wet Locations

Everything must be corrosion resistant (bolts, straps, etc.).

345-6 Size

The conduit used cannot be smaller than ½ in. or larger than 4 in.

345-7 Number of Conductors in Conduit

Refer to Chapter 9, Tables 1 and 4.

345-8 Reaming and Threading

All rough edges must be removed when the conduit is cut. When threaded in the field, a tapered cutting die must be used.

345-9 Couplings and Connectors

Threadless couplings and connectors can be used. Running threads cannot be used. Use concrete type in concrete and raintight in wet areas.

345-10 Bends—How Made

The conduit must not be injured. Refer to Table 346-10 for the radius of the inner edge for field bends. If the conduit does not have a lead sheath and the bend is made with a bending machine that uses one operation (one shot) the Table 346-10 Exception can be used.

TABLE 346-10 Radius of Conduit Bends (Inches)

Size of Conduit (In.)	*Conductors without Lead Sheath (In.)*	*Conductors with Lead Sheath (In.)*
½	4	6
¾	5	8
1	6	11
1¼	8	14

TABLE 346-10 (continued)

Size of Conduit (In.)	*Conductors without Lead Sheath (In.)*	*Conductors with Lead Sheath (In.)*
1½	10	16
2	12	21
2½	15	25
3	18	31
3½	21	36
4	24	40
4½	27	45
5	30	50
6	36	61

For SI units: (radius) 1 inch = 25.4 millimeters.

TABLE 346-10 Exception Radius of Conduit Bends (Inches)

Size of Conduit (In.)	*Radius to Center of Conduit (In.)*
½	4
¾	4½
1	5¾
1¼	7¼
1½	8¼
2	9½
2½	10½
3	13
3½	15
4	16
5	24
6	30

For SI units: (radius) 1 inch = 25.4 millimeters.

345-11 Bends—Number in One Run

The maximum that is permitted is not more than 360 degrees in bends between fittings or outlets, including those at the fittings or outlets.

345-12 Supports

The conduit must be supported at intervals no longer than 10 ft and fastened not more than 3 ft from a box, fitting, etc. There are two exceptions—under certain conditions with threaded couplings and in vertical risers.

345-13 Boxes and Fittings

Refer to Article 370.

345-14 Splices and Taps

They are permitted only in boxes or conduit bodies, not in the conduit. Refer to Article 370.

345-15 Bushings

A bushing must be used at the point where the conduit goes into a box, fitting, or other enclosure. This is to protect the wire. An exception is made if protection is provided with the box or fitting.

C. Construction Specifications

345-16 General

This type of conduit must be shipped in lengths of 10 ft with one coupling. Smaller lengths can be shipped but only for a special use. If the conduit is nonferrous of corrosion-resistant material, it must be marked to indicate it. The conduit must be marked every 2½ ft with the letters IMC.

ARTICLE 346
RIGID METAL CONDUIT

346-1 Use

Rigid metal conduit can be used in all locations and under all conditions, with the following provisos:

(a) If the conduit is steel and enamel coated, it can only be used indoors and not in highly corrosive areas.

(b) With the exception of aluminum fittings and enclosures and steel conduit, dissimilar metals in contact must not be used.

(c) It can be used in concrete, in contact with the earth, or in a corrosive area if properly protected and if it is suitable for that aim.

346-2 Other Articles

It must be in accordance with Article 300.

A. Installation

346-3 Cinder Fill

It cannot be used in or under cinder fill when there may be permanent moisture unless it is suitable for this type of installation, there are 2 in. or more of noncinder concrete all around it, and it is at least 18 in. under the fill.

346-4 Wet Locations

Everything must be corrosion-resistant (bolts, straps, etc.).

346-5 Minimum Size

One-half inch unless used for underplaster extensions (see Section 344-2) or enclosing motor leads [see Section 430-135(b)].

346-6 Number of Conductors in Conduit

Refer to chapter 9, Table 1.

346-7 Reaming and Threading

All rough edges must be removed when the conduit is cut. When threaded in the field, a tapered cutting die (¾ in. per foot taper) must be used.

346-8 Bushings

A bushing must be used at the point where the conduit goes into a box, fitting, or other enclosure. This is to protect the wire. An exception is made if protection is provided with the box or fitting.

346-9 Couplings and Connectors

Threadless couplings and connectors can be used. Running threads cannot be used. Use concrete type in concrete and raintight in wet areas.

346-10 Bends—How Made

The conduit must not be injured. Refer to Table 346-10 for the radius of the inner edge for field bends. If the conduit does not have a lead sheath and the bend is made with a bending machine that uses one operation, the Table 346-10 Exception can be used.

346-11 Bends—Number in One Run

The maximum that is permitted is not more than 360 degrees in bends between fittings or outlets, including those at the fittings or outlets.

346-12 Supports

The conduit must be supported at intervals no longer than 10 ft and fastened not more than 3 ft from a box, fitting, etc. An exception is made for straight runs with threaded couplings (refer to Table 346-12, page 70-230 in the *NEC*®). Another exception is made for vertical risers from items like machine tools, where the distance between supports can be increased to 20 ft if the conduit uses threaded couplings and is properly supported at the top and bottom. No stress is to be transmitted to the terminations.

346-13 Boxes and Fittings

Refer to Article 370.

346-14 Splices and Taps

They are permitted only in boxes or conduit bodies, not in the conduit. Refer to Article 370.

B. Construction Specifications

346-15 General

This type of conduit must be shipped in lengths of 10 ft with one coupling. Smaller lengths can be shipped but only for special use. If the conduit is nonferrous of corrosion-resistant material, it must be marked to indicate it. At every 10 ft the conduit must be marked with identification (refer to Section 110-21).

ARTICLE 347
RIGID NONMETALLIC CONDUIT

347-1 Description

This type of conduit is made from a nonmetallic material. It has to be able to withstand the load and impact in the installation being used (e.g., aboveground, underground, etc.) In addition, it must be moisture-resistant and resistant to chemical atmospheres and low temperature and sunlight, and flame-retardant if used aboveground. Some of the materials that have been accepted are fiber, asbestos cement, and polyethylene for underground use and rigid PVC for both underground and aboveground use.

347-2 Uses Permitted

Some of the uses permitted and other references in the *NEC*® are: in walls, floors, ceilings, and cinder fill, exposed when not subject to injury and approved; in corrosive locations where approved for that type of location and in accordance with Section 300-6; in dry and damp locations in accordance with Section 347-3; in wet locations where the material is approved; and underground in accordance with Sections 300-5 and 710-3(b).

347-3 Uses Not Permitted

This type of conduit must not be used in hazardous locations except where permitted by Sections 514-8, 515-5, and the Exception to Section 501-4(b); in areas where there might be physical damage to the conduit; in areas where the ambient temperature or the insulation temperature will be greater than allowed for the conduit and for supporting fixtures or equipment.

347-4 Other Articles

It must be in accordance with Article 300. If equipment grounding is necessary (Article 250), a separate wire must be installed in the conduit.

A. Installation

347-5 Trimming

Remove rough edges on cuts.

347-6 Joints

Use approved methods.

347-8 Supports

Refer to Table 347-8, page 70-232 in the *NEC*®, for spacing of supports. There must be a support no farther than 3 ft from a termination point.

347-9 Expansion Joints

Use approved type where necessary.

347-10 Minimum Size—½ Inch

347-11 Number of Conductors

Refer to Chapter 9, Table 1.

347-12 Bushings

A bushing must be used at the point where the conduit goes into a box or fitting unless protection is provided in the box or fitting.

347-13 Bends—How Made

The conduit must not be injured. Refer to Table 346-10.

347-14 Bends—Number in One Run

The maximum that is permitted is not more than 360 degrees in bends between fittings or outlets, including those at the fittings or outlets.

347-15 Boxes and Fittings

Refer to Article 370.

347-16 Splices and Taps

They are permitted only in boxes or conduit bodies, not in the conduit. Refer to Article 370.

B. Construction Specifications

347-17 General

The conduit must be marked with identification every 10 ft (refer to Section 110-21).

ARTICLE 348 ELECTRICAL METALLIC TUBING

348-1 Use

This type of tubing (sometimes called EMT) can be installed either exposed or concealed in most locations except under the following conditions: if it will be subject to severe damage; if the corrosion-resistant substance is enamel; in cinder fill or cinder concrete where there will always be moisture unless the tubing is 18 in. or more under the fill or protected by at least 2 in. of noncinder concrete on all sides. With the exception of aluminum fittings and enclosures and steel conduit, dissimilar metals in contact must not be used, where avoidable. The reader is cautioned to refer to Articles 500 through 516 for hazardous areas where this type of tubing is allowed. It is not permitted in most hazardous locations.

348-2 Other Articles

It must be in accordance with Article 300.

A. Installation

348-4 Wet Locations

Everything must be corrosion-resistant (bolts, straps, etc.).

348-5 Size

The minimum size permitted is ½ in. unless used for underplaster extensions (see Section 344-2) or enclosing motor leads [see Section 430-145(b)]. The maximum size permitted is 4 in.

348-6 Number of Conductors in Tubing

Refer to Chapter 9, Table 1.

348-7 Threads

Threading is not permitted except on factory-threaded integral couplings.

348-8 Couplings and Connectors

They must be tight and concrete-tight if used in concrete and raintight if used in wet locations.

348-9 Bends—How Made

The tubing must not be injured. Refer to Table 346-10 for the radius of the inner edge of a field bend. When using a machine in the field designed for bending, Table 346-10 Exception can be used.

348-10 Bends—Number in One Run

The maximum that is permitted is not more than 360 degrees in bends between fittings or outlets, including those at the fittings or outlets.

348-11 Reaming

Remove rough edges of all cuts.

348-12 Supports

The tubing must be fastened at intervals no longer than 10 ft and not more than 3 ft from a box, fitting, etc.

348-13 Boxes and Fittings

Refer to Article 370.

348-14 Splices and Taps

They are permitted only in boxes or conduit bodies, not in the tubing. Refer to Article 370.

B. Construction Specifications

348-15 General

The tubing and its fittings must be circular in cross section. It must be finished so that it can be distinguished from rigid metal conduit after its installation. If threaded couplings are used (when permitted), they must not bend the tubing at the threads.

ARTICLE 349
FLEXIBLE METALLIC TUBING

349-1 Scope

This tubing is circular, flexible, metallic, and liquidtight without a nonmetallic jacket. It can be used where there is no possibility of physical damage.

349-2 Other Articles

It must be in accordance with Article 300.

349-3 Uses Permitted

This type of tubing can be used in dry locations, and in acccessible locations if not subject to damage or concealed, on branch circuits, and not more than 1000 V.

349-4 Uses Not Permitted

It cannot be used in hoistways, storage battery rooms, hazardous locations, embedded in concrete, or directly buried in the earth. Lengths larger than 6 ft are not permitted.

B. Construction and Installation

349-10 Size

The minimum size permitted is ½ in. except that ⅜ in. can be used in accordance with Section 300-22(b) and (c) or part of an approved lighting fixture assembly in accordance with Section 410-67(c) and not more than 6 ft in length. The maximum size permitted is ¾ in.

349-12 Number of Conductors

Refer to Chapter 9, Table 1, for the number of conductors permitted in ½- and ¾-in. tubing. Refer to Table 350-3, page 70-228 of the *NEC*®, for the number of conductors permitted in ⅜-in. tubing.

349-16 Grounding

Refer to Section 250-91 (b), Exception No. 1.

349-18 Fittings

349-20 Bends

If the tubing is bent infrequently after installation, refer to Table 349-20(a), in the *NEC*®. If the tubing is bent for installation, use Table 349-20(b), in the *NEC*®.

ARTICLE 350
FLEXIBLE METAL CONDUIT

350-1 Other Articles

It must be installed in accordance with Articles 300, 333, and 346.

350-2 Use

This type of conduit cannot be used in wet locations (except if approved for a wet location or if it has a lead covering, and water probably will not enter the enclosure that the conduit is connected to), in hoistways (exceptions listed in Section 620-21), in storage battery rooms, in classified hazardous locations [exceptions listed in Section 501-4(b)], if rubber-covered and near a material that will deteriorate rubber, and if underground or in aggregate or poured concrete.

350-3 Minimum Size

The minimum size permitted is ½ in. Five exceptions to this are for underplaster extension (refer to Section 344-2, where permitted); enclosing motor leads [refer to Section 430-145(b)]; for a length not longer than 6 ft if part of an assembly, tap connection to, or part of a lighting fixture, where ⅜-in. conduit can be used; flexible metal conduit ⅜ in. for manufactured wiring system in accordance with Section 604-6(a); and where allowed in Section 620-21, Exception No. 5.

350-4 Supports

This type of conduit must be secured within 12 in. from a box, cabinet, or fitting and every 4½ ft. Three exceptions to this are if the length is a fixture tap (not more than 6 ft), if the conduit is fished, or if it is a length not in excess of 3 ft from a terminal.

350-5 Grounding

This type of conduit can be used as a means of grounding if it has been approved for grounding. Refer to the *NEC*® for exceptions.

350-6 Bends

The maximum that is permitted is not more than 360 degrees in bends between fittings or outlets, including those at the fittings or outlets.

ARTICLE 351
LIQUIDTIGHT FLEXIBLE METAL CONDUIT AND LIQUIDTIGHT FLEXIBLE NONMETALLIC CONDUIT

A. Liquidtight Flexible Metal Conduit

351-1 Scope

351-2 Definition

This conduit is similar to flexible metal conduit, but it has a jacket over the metal conduit. The jacket is liquidtight, nonmetallic, and sunlight-resistant.

351-3 Other Articles

It must be installed in accordance with Articles 300, 350, 501, 502, 503, and 553, where applicable.

351-4 Use

This conduit can be installed exposed or concealed, and directly buried in earth if protection from liquids, vapor, or solids is necessary or if flexibility is desired. It can be installed in hazardous areas if approved for that installation. Refer to Sections 501-4(b), 502-4, 503-3 and 553-7(b). It cannot be installed when subject to damage or where temperatures exceed that which is approved for the material.

351-5 Size

Minimum ½ in. For exceptions, refer to Section 350-3. The maximum size allowed is 4 in.

351-6 Number of Conductors

Refer to Chapter 9, Table 1. For ⅜-in. conduit refer to Table 350-3 in the *NEC*®.

351-7 Fittings

351-8 Supports

The same as with flexible metal conduit (see Section 350-4).

351-9 Grounding

This type of conduit can be used as a means of grounding if it has been approved for grounding. Refer to the *NEC®* for exceptions.

351-10 Bends

The maximum that is permitted is not more than 360 degrees in bends between fittings or outlets, including those at the fittings or outlets.

B. Liquidtight Flexible Nonmetallic Conduit

351-22 Definition

This conduit has a smooth inner surface and reinforcement in the conduit wall. It is all made of nonmetallic material. The conduit is flame-resistant. It is used for industrial applications.

351-23 Use

This conduit can be installed exposed if protection from vapors, liquids, or solids is necessary or if flexibility is desired. It cannot be installed if subject to damage, when temperatures will exceed those for which the conduit is approved, in lengths in excess of 6 ft, and where voltages higher than 600 V are used. It can also be used outdoors when listed and suitable.

351-24 Size

½ to 2 in. For leads of motors ⅜ in. can be used in accordance with Section 430-145(b).

351-25 Number of Conductors

Refer to Chapter 9, Table 1.

351-26 Fittings

351-27 Grounding

If required, install a separate wire inside or outside of conduit. Refer to *NEC®* for restrictions.

ARTICLE 352
SURFACE METAL RACEWAYS AND SURFACE NONMETALLIC RACEWAYS

A. Surface Metal Raceways

352-1 Use

This can be installed in dry areas. It cannot be installed where it might be damaged, where there are corrosive vapors, in hoistways, where the voltage between conductors is 300 V or more unless the metal is at least 0.04 in., in a hazardous area [refer to Section 501-4(b) for an exception], or concealed. It can be installed concealed for an underplaster extension or where permitted by Section 645-2(c)(2).

352-2 Other Articles

It must be installed in accordance with Article 300.

352-3 Size of Conductors

They cannot be larger than the raceway was designed for.

352-4 Number of Conductors in Raceways

Refer to design criteria. Exceptions to the use of derating factors are noted in the *NEC*® in this paragraph.

352-5 Extension through Walls and Floors

This can be done if the material is dry and no joints are in the extension.

352-6 Combination Raceways

352-7 Splices and Taps

352-8 Construction

B. Surface Nonmetallic Raceways

352-21 Description

This raceway is similar to the metallic type except that it is made of nonmetallic material that is resistant to moisture atmospheres, chemical atmospheres, impact and crushing, distortion from heat, and low temperatures. It is also flame-retardant.

352-22 Use

This can be used in dry areas. It cannot be installed concealed, where it might be damaged, where the voltage between conductors is 300 V or more, in hoistways, in a hazardous area [refer to Section 501-4(b) for an exception], if ambient temperatures are higher than 50°C, or for conductors with insulation temperatures higher than 75°C.

352-23 Other Articles

It must be installed in accordance with Article 300.

352-24 Size of Conductors

Refer to Section 352-3.

352-25 Number of Conductors in Raceways

This is the same as Section 352-4.

352-26 Combination Raceways

352-27 General

ARTICLE 353 MULTIOUTLET ASSEMBLY

353-1 Other Articles

353-2 Use

353-3 Metal Multioutlet Assembly through Dry Partitions

ARTICLE 354
UNDERFLOOR RACEWAYS

354-1 Other Articles

354-2 Use

This type of raceway can be used in an office in the concrete floor or other floorings. It cannot be used if exposed to corrosive vapors, in a hazardous area [for an exception refer to Section 501-4(b)], in concrete, or in corrosive areas unless properly protected and approved.

354-3 Covering

354-4 Size of Conductors

Not larger than designed for.

354-5 Maximum Number of Conductors in Raceway

Not more than 40% fill.

354-6 Splices and Taps

354-7 Discontinued Outlets

354-8 Laid in Straight Lines

354-9 Marker at Ends

354-10 Dead Ends

354-13 Junction Boxes

354-14 Inserts

354-15 Connections to Cabinets and Walls

ARTICLE 356
CELLULAR METAL FLOOR RACEWAYS

356-1 Definition

This is a raceway system that is part of the entire floor and installed as such. A complete definition of terms is given in the *NEC*®.

356-2 Use

356-3 Other Articles

A. Installation

356-4 Size of Conductors

Not larger than 1/0 unless special permission is obtained.

356-5 Maximum Number of Conductors in Raceway

Not more than 40% fill.

356-6 Splices and Taps

356-7 Discontinued Outlets

356-8 Markers

356-9 Junction Boxes

356-10 Inserts

356-11 Connection to Cabinets and Extensions from Cells

B. Construction Specifications

356-12 General

The following article titles are listed for reference:

Article 358—Cellular Concrete Floor Raceways; **Article 362**—Wireways; **Article 363**—Flat Cable Assemblies—Type FC; **Article 364**—Busways; **Article 365**—Cablebus; **Article 366**—Electrical Floor Assemblies.

ARTICLE 370
OUTLET, DEVICE, PULL AND JUNCTION BOXES, CONDUIT BODIES AND FITTINGS

A. Scope and General

370-1 Scope

Special requirements for installations over 600 V are indicated in Part D.

370-2 Round Boxes

These are not permitted if locknuts or bushings are required on the side of the box.

370-3 Nonmetallic Boxes

These are only to be used with nonmetallic cable or conduit, open wire installations, electrical nonmetallic tubing, or knob-and-tube wiring. They can be used with metal raceway or cable only if the box is over 100 cubic inches with a means for bonding.

370-4 Metal Boxes

These must be grounded as provided in Article 250.

B. Installation

370-5 Damp, Wet Locations, or Hazardous (Classified) Locations

Moisture must be prevented from getting into the box. They must be listed for use in wet locations. When installed in a hazardous location, conform to Articles 500 through 517.

370-6 Number of Conductors in Outlet, Device and Junction Boxes, and Conduit Bodies

Table 370-6(a) of the *NEC*® indicates the maximum number of conductors of a single size that can be

used in a box. If additional devices are used, such as studs, clamps, or hickeys, each type of device counts as a conductor; each strap counts as a conductor, and all grounding conductors count as one conductor. If a conductor runs through the box, it is figured as one conductor, as is each conductor entering and terminating in the box. Conductors that do not go out of the box are not counted. If the wire sizes are not the same, Table 370-6(b) is used. Table 370-6(b) is also used for other boxes not listed in Table 370-6(a).
Refer to this section of the Code for a complete description.

370-7 Conductors Entering Boxes, Conduit Bodies or Fittings

All openings must be closed. All conductors coming into a box, conduit body or fitting must be protected against abrasion. Special requirements are indicated with open wiring or concealed knob-and-tube wiring. If cable or raceway is used the cable or raceway must be fastened to the box, conduit body or fitting. Refer to Section 370-7 of the *NEC*®, for all rules and to Section 373-6(c) for wire No. 4 or larger.

370-8 Unused Openings

These openings must be closed. When metal plugs are used in nonmetallic boxes, they must be recessed at least ¼ in.

370-9 Boxes Enclosing Flush Devices

They must be closed on the back and sides and a support for the device (usually a stud or screw hole) must be in the box. The screw that supports the box cannot be used to attach the device.

370-10 In Wall or Ceiling

When the box is set in noncombustible material, it can be set back as much as ¼ in. When it is

TABLE 370-6(a) Metal Boxes

Box Dimension, Inches Trade Size or Type	*Min. Cu. In. Cap.*	*Maximum Number of Conductors*						
		No. 18	*No. 16*	*No. 14*	*No. 12*	*No. 10*	*No. 8*	*No. 6*
4 × 1¼ round or octagonal	12.5	8	7	6	5	5	4	0
4 × 1½ round or octagonal	15.5	10	8	7	6	6	5	0
4 × 2⅛ round or octagonal	21.5	14	12	10	9	8	7	0
4 × 1¼ square	18.0	12	10	9	8	7	6	0
4 × 1½ square	21.0	14	12	10	9	8	7	0
4 × 2⅛ square	30.3	20	17	15	13	12	10	6*
4¹¹⁄₁₆ × 1¼ square	25.5	17	14	12	11	10	8	0
4¹¹⁄₁₆ × 1½ square	29.5	19	16	14	13	11	9	0
4¹¹⁄₁₆ × 2⅛ square	42.0	28	24	21	18	16	14	6
3 × 2 × 1½ device	7.5	5	4	3	3	3	2	0
3 × 2 × 2 device	10.0	6	5	5	4	4	3	0
3 × 2 × 2¼ device	10.5	7	6	5	4	4	3	0

3 × 2 × 2½ device	12.5	8	7	6	5	5	4	0
3 × 2 × 2¾ device	14.0	9	8	7	6	5	4	0
3 × 2 × 3½ device	18.0	12	10	9	8	7	6	0
4 × 2⅛ × 1½ device	10.3	6	5	5	4	4	3	0
4 × 2⅛ × 1⅞ device	13.0	8	7	6	5	5	4	0
4 × 2⅛ × 2⅛ device	14.5	9	8	7	6	5	4	0
3¾ × 2 × 2½ masonry box/gang	14.0	9	8	7	6	5	4	0
3¾ × 2 × 3½ masonry box/gang	21.0	14	12	10	9	8	7	0
FS—minimum internal depth 1¾ single cover/gang	13.5	9	7	6	6	5	4	0
FD—minimum internal depth 2⅜ single cover/gang	18.0	12	10	9	8	7	6	3
FS—minimum internal depth 1¾ multiple cover/gang	18.0	12	10	9	8	7	6	0
FD—minimum internal depth 2⅜ multiple cover/gang	24.0	16	13	12	10	9	8	4

* Not to be used as a pull box. For termination only.

TABLE 370-6(b) Volume Required per Conductor

Size of Conductor	*Free Space within Box for each Conductor*
No. 18	1.5 cubic inches
No. 16	1.75 cubic inches
No. 14	2. cubic inches
No. 12	2.25 cubic inches
No. 10	2.5 cubic inches
No. 8	3. cubic inches
No. 6	5. cubic inches

set in combustible material, it has to be flush with the finished surface.

370-11 Repairing Plaster and Drywall or Plasterboard

370-12 Exposed Surface Extensions

370-13 Supports

This section details methods of support. It indicates where they are needed and what can be used.

370-14 Depth of Outlet Boxes

370-15 Covers and Canopies

370-17 Outlet Boxes

They must be designed for the purpose to be used (i.e., floor or lighting fixture). A fixture support must be in a lighting fixture box. Cannot be used as sole support for ceiling paddle fans unless listed for that purpose.

370-18 Pull and Junction Boxes

(a) Minimum Size. The following rules apply only when the raceway is ¾ in. or larger and the wire is No. 4 or larger. In a straight pull, the box must be at least 8 times the trade diameter of the largest raceway in length. When angle pulls or U-pulls are used, the distance between the raceway entrances and the opposite wall must be at least 6 times the trade diameter of the largest raceway. In addition, that distance must be increased by the diameter of each additional raceway in any one row on the same wall of the box. Two raceways that enclose the same conductor cannot be closer than 6 times the trade diameter of the larger raceway. There is an exception where the entry is opposite a removable cover. There is also an exception if the conduit does not have its maximum fill.

(b) Conductors in Pull or Junction Boxes

(c) Covers

(d) Permanent Barriers. If a permanent barrier is in a box, each section is considered a box.

370-19 Junction, Pull, and Outlet Boxes to Be Accessible

C. Construction Specifications

370-20 Metal Boxes, Conduit Bodies, and Fittings

370-21 Covers

370-22 Bushings

370-23 Nonmetallic Boxes

370-24 Marking

D. Pull and Junction Boxes for Use on Systems Over 600 Volts, Nominal

370-50 General

370-51 Size of Pull and Junction Boxes

370-52 Construction and Installation Requirements

ARTICLE 373
CABINETS AND CUTOUT BOXES

373-1 Scope

A. Installation

373-2 Damp, Wet, or Hazardous (Classified) Locations

When installed in wet locations, they must be weatherproof. In damp or wet locations, surface boxes must prevent moisture from entering and have at least ¼ in. of air space between it and the wall or support. In hazardous locations conformance must be made with the requirements of Articles 500 through 517.

373-3 Position in Wall

When installed in noncombustible material, they may be set back ¼ in. When installed in combustible material, they must be flush with the surface.

373-4 Unused Openings

These must be closed. When metal plugs are used in nonmetallic boxes, they must be recessed at least ¼ in.

373-5 Conductors Entering Cabinets or Cutout Boxes

The opening must be closed. When metal cabinets or boxes are used with open wiring or knob and tube work, the conductor must come in through a bushing. In dry areas, it may enter through flexible tubing. Cables must be secured to the box.

373-6 Deflection of Conductors

Refer to pages 70-267 and 70-268 in the *NEC*® for minimum width of gutters and bending spaces.

373-7 Space in Enclosure

373-8 Enclosures for Switches or Overcurrent Devices

373-9 Side or Back Wiring Spaces or Gutters

B. Construction Specifications

373-10 Material

If metal, it must have corrosion protection. Sheet steel cabinets must be at least 0.053 in. uncoated. Nonmetallic cabinets must be approved by the authorities.

373-11 Spacing

ARTICLE 374
AUXILIARY GUTTERS

374-1 Use

374-2 Extension beyond Equipment

It must not extend more than 30 ft from the equipment it supplements.

374-3 Supports

374-4 Covers

374-5 Number of Conductors

Not more than 30 conductors are allowed at any point and the area of the conductors cannot be more than 20% of the area of the gutter. There are three exceptions to this: (1) for elevators; (2) for signaling or motor controller circuits; and (3) when the derating factors are used for ampacity of conductors, the 30-conductor limit does not apply.

374-6 Ampacity of Conductors

When there are not more than 30 current-carrying conductors, the derating factors for ampacities do not have to be applied. The capacities of bars cannot exceed 1000 A per square inch for copper and 700 A per square inch for aluminum.

374-7 Clearance of Bare Live Parts

374-8 Splices and Taps

374-9 Construction and Installation

ARTICLE 380
SWITCHES

380-1 Scope

380-2 Switch Connections

Three- and four-way switches must be installed so that switching is in the ungrounded conductor. If the wiring is installed in metal enclosures, it must be in accordance with the requirements of Section 300-20(a). A grounded conductor must not be switched. There are two exceptions to this.

380-3 Enclosure

380-4 Wet Locations

380-5 Time Switches, Flashers and Similar Devices

380-6 Position of Knife Switches

380-7 Indicating

380-8 Accessibility and Grouping

380-9 Faceplates for Flush-Mounted Snap Switches

380-10 Mounting of Snap Switches

380-11 Circuit Breakers as Switches

380-12 Grounding of Enclosures

380-13 Knife Switches

380-14 Rating and Use of Snap Switches

B. Construction Specifications

380-15 Marking

They must be marked with current, voltage, and the maximum horsepower if horsepower rated.

380-16 600-Volt Knife Switches

380-17 Fused Switches

Parallel fusing is not permitted.

380-18 Wire Bending Space

ARTICLE 384 SWITCHBOARDS AND PANELBOARDS

384-1 General

Switchboards, panelboards, distribution boards, and battery-charging panels are covered.

384-2 Other Articles

Articles 240, 250, 370, and 380 and applicable sections of other Code articles must be complied with.

384-3 Support and Arrangement of Busbars and Conductors

They must be located to be free from damage and be secured. They must be arranged to avoid overheating due to induction. When used as service equipment, a grounding bar must be provided and it must be bonded to the case and frame. Locations of terminals must be so as to avoid the necessity of reaching across ungrounded line bars. In a four-wire delta system the bar or conductor with the highest voltage to ground must be marked and it must be the B phase. Three-phase buses must have the phases A, B, C, front to back, left to right, or top to bottom when looking from the front. There is an exception for equipment in the same switchboard or panelboard as the meter. Refer to Section 373-6 for minimum wire bending space.

384-4 Installation

No piping, ducts, equipment, etc., can pass through the room or space designated for a switchboard or panelboard. There are four exceptions to this noted in the *NEC*®.

A. Switchboards

384-5 Location of Switchboards

384-6 Wet Locations

384-7 Location Relative to Easily Ignitable Material

384-8 Clearances

At least 3 ft to a combustible ceiling. Refer to Section 110-16 for clearances around the switchboard.

384-9 Conductor Insulation

384-10 Clearance for Conductors Entering Bus Enclosure

384-11 Grounding Switchboard Frames

They must be grounded.

384-12 Grounding of Instruments, Relays, Meters, and Instrument Transformers on Switchboards

Refer to Sections 250-121 through 250-125.

B. Panelboards

384-13 General

They must have current, voltage, phase, and manufacturer's trademark markings visible after installation. The rating must not be less than the feeder capacity.

384-14 Lighting and Appliance Branch-Circuit Panelboard

If a panelboard has more than 10% of its overcurrent devices rated less than 30 A with a neutral connection, it falls into this category.

384-15 Number of Overcurrent Devices on One Panelboard

Not more than 42 overcurrent devices can be installed in a lighting or appliance branch-circuit panelboard. This does not include mains. Each pole of a multipole circuit breaker is considered a single circuit.

384-16 Overcurrent Protection

(a) Individual overcurrent protection must be provided for a lighting and appliance branch-circuit panelboard of not more than two sets of circuit breakers or fuses. The overcurrent protection cannot exceed the ratings of the panelboard. This is not required if the feeder has overcurrent protection that does not exceed the rating of the panelboard. If an existing panelboard is used as service equipment in a single-residence occupancy, the individual protection is not required.

(b) Overcurrent protection not greater than 200 A is required for a panelboard that has snap switches rated 30 A or less.

(c) Where the load will continue for at least 3 hours on an overcurrent device in the panelboard, the load cannot be greater than 80% of the device's rating. This is not required if the assembly and the device are rated for 100% continuous duty.

(d) For panelboards that are supplied through a transformer, the overcurrent protection required must be on the secondary of the transformer. This is not required for two-wire secondaries (single voltage). Refer to Section 450-3(b)(1).

(e) A panelboard with less than three-phase

buses cannot use a three-phase overcurrent device or disconnect.

384-17 Panelboards in Damp or Wet Locations

Refer to Section 373-2(a).

384-18 Enclosure

Panelboards must be in some type of enclosure with a dead front. If only qualified persons have access to the panelboards, dead fronts are not required.

384-19 Relative Arrangement of Switches and Fuses

Fuses must be installed on the load side of switches.

C. Construction Specifications

384-20 Panels

Must be made of moisture-resistant noncombustible material for switchboards.

384-21 Busbars

Must be rigidly mounted.

384-22 Protection of Instrument Circuits

Instruments must be protected and the rating must not exceed 15 A.

384-23 Component Parts

They must be in accordance with Articles 240 and 380.

384-24 Knife Switches

384-25 Wire Bending Space in Panelboards

Top and bottom wire bending space must be in accordance with Table 373-6(b). Side bending space must be in accordance with Table 373-6(a). Refer to this article in the *NEC*® for exceptions.

384-26 Minimum Spacings

Refer to Table 384-26.

384-27 Grounding of Panelboards

Panelboards must be grounded and in accordance with Article 250 or Section 384-3(c). When nonmetallic cable or raceway is used, a grounding terminal bar must be installed and kept separate from the neutral bar. The grounding terminal does not have to be separated from the neutral bar at separate buildings in accordance with Section 250-24. An isolated ground conductor can pass through the panelboard with connection to the ground bar in accordance with Section 250-74.

4

EQUIPMENT FOR GENERAL USE

ARTICLE 400 FLEXIBLE CORDS AND CABLES

A. General

400-1 Scope

400-2 Other Articles

400-3 Suitability

400-4 Types

Table 400-4 lists the approved types of flexible cables and cords. A cable or cord not on this list must have a special investigation. Notes to the table should be reviewed.

400-5 Ampacity of Flexible Cords and Cables

Table 400-5 shows the ampacity of up to three current-carrying conductors. When more than three current-carrying conductors are used, a derating of the values in Table 400-5 as follows:

4–6	80%
7–24	70%
24–42	60%
43 and above	50%

400-6 Marking

400-7 Uses Permitted

(1) Pendants; (2) wiring of fixtures; (3) connection of portable lamps or appliances; (4) for elevator cables; (5) cranes and hoists; (6) for stationary equipment if they are to be moved a lot; (7) to prevent noise and vibration transmission; (8) where removal for maintenance is required; (9) for data processing cables (refer to Section 645-2); (10) connection of moving parts; (11) as allowed in Sections 305-2(b) and 305-2(c) for the connection of moving parts. When used as indicated in (3), (6), and (8), a plug must be used on the cord and it must be plugged into a receptacle for power.

400-8 Uses Not Permitted

(1) Fixed wiring of a building; (2) installed through a hole in walls, ceilings, or floors; (3) through doorways, windows, or similar openings; (4) installed concealed; (5) attached to building surfaces.

400-9 Splices

400-10 Pull at Joints and Terminals

Some type of strain relief must be provided (i.e., a knot, tape, or special fitting).

400-11 In Show Windows and Show Cases

Use only Type S, SO, SE, SEO, SOO, SJ, SJE, SJO, SJEO, SJOO, ST, STO, STOO, SJT, SJTO, SJTOO, or AFS. This restriction is not necessary for chain-supported lighting fixtures or portable lamps and display merchandise.

400-12 Minimum Size

Refer to Table 400-4.

400-13 Overcurrent Protection

If not smaller than No. 18 or tinsel cords or a cord approved for a specific appliance, no separate overcurrent protection is required.

400-14 Protection from Damage

B. Construction Specifications

400-20 Labels

400-21 Nominal Insulation Thickness

Refer to Table 400-4.

400-22 Grounded-Conductor Identification

One conductor that is used as a grounded circuit conductor must be clearly marked. Identification methods include (1) a white or gray braid, (2) a tracer of a distinguishable color in the braid, (3) white or gray insulation, (4) white or gray separator, (5) tinned conductor, and (6) some distinguishable surface marking.

400-23 Grounding-Conductor Identification

This conductor must also have a distinguishing marking of a colored braid, colored insulation, or colored cover. The color to be used is either green or green with yellow stripes.

400-24 Attachment Plugs

C. Portable Cables Over 600 Volts, Nominal

400-30 Scope

400-31 Construction

400-32 Shielding

400-33 Grounding

400-34 Minimum Bending Radii

400-35 Fittings

400-36 Splices and Terminations

ARTICLE 402
FIXTURE WIRES

402-1 Scope

402-2 Other Articles

402-3 Types

Refer to Table 402-3 for those types permitted. They can be used at 600 V.

402-5 Ampacities of Fixture Wires

No. 18: 6 A; No. 16: 8 A; No. 14: 17 A; No. 12: 23 A; and No. 10: 28 A.

402-6 Minimum Size

Not smaller than No. 18.

402-7 Number of Conductors in Conduit

Refer to Chapter 9, Table 2.

402-8 Grounded Conductor Identification

402-9 Marking

402-10 Uses Permitted

Lighting fixtures and similar equipment where enclosed and protected and for connecting lighting fixtures to branch circuits.

402-11 Uses Not Permitted

Cannot be used as branch-circuit conductors except in accordance with Sections 725-16 and 760-16.

402-12 Overcurrent Protection

ARTICLE 410
LIGHTING FIXTURES, LAMPHOLDERS, LAMPS, RECEPTACLES, AND ROSETTES

A. General

410-1 Scope

410-2 Application to Other Articles

410-3 Live Parts

B. Fixture Locations

410-4 Fixtures in Specific Locations

(a) Wet and Damp Locations. The fixtures must be installed in a manner so that water will not enter or collect in the lampholder, wireway, etc. Examples of wet locations are underground, in concrete slabs, where it can be saturated with water, etc. Examples of damp locations are partially protected areas such as under canopies, roofs, or interiors, where subject to moisture, as in farms.

(b) Corrosive Locations

(c) In Ducts or Hoods. This location is permitted only in nonresidential cooking areas and is subject to four specific conditions.

(d) Pendants

410-5 Fixtures near Combustible Material

The fixture construction must ensure that the combustible material will not be subjected to temperatures over 194°F.

410-6 Fixtures over Combustible Material

These must be unswitched fixtures. The lampholder must be at least 8 ft above the floor unless an individual switch is installed for each fixture.

410-7 Fixtures in Show Windows

External wiring is not permitted except chain-supported fixtures.

410-8 Fixtures in Clothes Closets

They may be installed as follows:

1. On the wall above the door when there is at least 18 in. of clearance between the fixture and combustible material.
2. On the ceilings when there is no obstruction to the floor and at least 18 in. clearance horizontally to combustible material.

A flush fixture or ceiling-mounted fluorescent fixture can be installed provided that it has a solid lens and there is at least 6 in. clearance between the fixture and storage. Pendant fixtures are not permitted.

410-9 Space for Cove Lighting

C. Provisions at Fixture Outlet Boxes, Canopies, and Pans

410-10 Space for Conductors

410-11 Temperature Limit of Conductors in Outlet Boxes

410-12 Outlet Boxes to be Covered

410-13 Covering of Combustible Material at Outlet Boxes

410-14 Connection of Electric-Discharge Lighting Fixtures

D. Fixture Supports

410-15 Supports—General

410-16 Means of Support

The *NEC®* specifies a few requirements for outlet boxes, inspection, suspended ceilings, fixture studs, insulating joints, raceway fittings, and busways. One important requirement to note is that a fixture that weighs more than 50 lbs. cannot be supported from an outlet box. It must be independently supported.

E. Grounding

410-17 General

410-18 Exposed Fixture Parts

If the wiring system provides a means of grounding, exposed conductive parts must be grounded. If no provision for grounding is available, they must be insulated.

410-19 Equipment Over 150 Volts to Ground

All metal fixtures, transformers, and transformer enclosures must be grounded. All other metal parts must be insulated or grounded.

410-20 Equipment Grounding Conductor Attachment

A means to connect an equipment ground must be provided for a metal fixture.

410-21 Methods of Grounding

Mechanical connection to an equipment grounding conductor in accordance with Sections 250-91(b) and 250-95.

F. Wiring of Fixture

410-22 Fixture Wiring—General

410-23 Polarization of Fixtures

410-24 Conductors

410-25 Conductors for Certain Conditions

410-27 Pendant Conductors for Incandescent Filament Lamps

410-28 Protection of Conductors and Insulation

410-29 Cord-Connected Showcases

410-30 Cord-Connected Lampholders and Fixtures

410-31 Fixtures as Raceways

Normally, fixtures cannot be used as raceways. It is permitted, however, if the fixture is listed for that use, when the fixtures are designed for end-to-end assembly. Only two two-wire circuits are permitted. If the branch-circuit conductors come within 3 in. of a ballast, the wire must have a usage rating of at least 194°F.

G. Construction of Fixtures

410-34 Combustible Shades and Enclosures

410-35 Fixture Rating

410-36 Design and Material

410-37 Nonmetallic Fixtures

410-38 Mechanical Strength

410-39 Wiring Space

410-42 Portable Lamps

410-44 Cord Bushings

410-45 Tests

410-46 Live Parts

H. Installation of Lampholders

410-47 Screw-Shell Type

410-48 Double-Pole Switched Lampholders

410-49 Lampholders in Wet or Damp Locations

J. Construction of Lampholders

410-50 Insulation

410-51 Lead Wires

410-52 Switched Lampholders

K. Lamps and Auxiliary Equipment

410-53 Bases, Incandescent Lamps

410-54 Electric-Discharge Lamp Auxiliary Equipment

410-55 Arc Lamp

L. Receptacles, Cord Connectors, and Attachment Plugs (Caps)

410-56 Rating and Type

Receptacles cannot be used as lampholders and must be rated at least 15 A 125 V or 15 A 250 V. This section also specifies requirements for CO/ALR receptacles, faceplates, position of receptacle faces, attachment plugs, attachment plug ejectors, mechanisms, noninterchangeability, and conductors. One thing to note is that the receptacle must project at least 0.015 in. from a metal faceplate.

410-57 Receptacles in Damp or Wet Locations

Receptacles located in damp areas must have a weatherproof enclosure. The receptacle need only be protected when it is covered, not when it is in use. Receptacles located in wet locations must be weatherproof-protected at all times, even when in use. An exception to the wet location rule is made only if portable tools or plug-in devices are used that will not be left plugged in when not in use. In these cases, the protection provided for damp locations is acceptable. Receptacles located outdoors must be installed high enough so that water will not touch the plate or receptacle (snow or water accumulation). Floor receptacles must be installed so as not to be damaged by cleaning equipment. If the receptacle is flush-mounted, the faceplate must provide the weatherproofing (gasketing, etc.)

410-58 Grounding-Type Receptacles, Adapters, Cord Connectors, and Attachment Plugs.

Grounding-type receptacles must have a grounding slot. Grounding-type plugs must have a grounding prong and this prong must make contact first. The ground pole must be distinctively marked and it must not be used for any other purpose.

M. Rosettes

410-59 Unapproved Types

410-60 Rosettes in Damp or Wet Locations

410-61 Rating

410-62 Rosettes for Exposed Wiring

410-63 Rosettes for Use with Boxes or Raceways

N. Special Provisions for Flush and Recessed Fixtures

410-64 General

This type of fixture must comply with Sections 410-65 through 410-72 as well as other parts of the *NEC®*.

410-65 Temperature

They must be installed so that any adjacent combustible material will not be subjected to a temperature higher than 194°F. If the fixture is recessed in fire-resistant construction in a fire-resistant building, the temperature restriction is increased to 302°F if the fixture is approved for this service. All recessed incandescent fixtures must have thermal protection. This restriction is not required if the fixture is installed in poured concrete and is approved for this use or when the fixture is listed and by construction design provides thermally protected characteristics.

410-66 Clearance and Installation

Recessed parts of the fixture must be at least ½ in. from combustible material and at least 3 in. from thermal insulation unless the fixture is approved for direct contact with the insulation or are recessed fluorescent fixtures.

410-67 Wiring

The insulation used on conductors must be suitable for the temperatures that they will be subjected to. Tap conductors can run to a box at least 1 ft from the fixture. The raceway used for the tap conductor must be at least 4 ft long and not more than 6 ft long.

P. Construction of Flush and Recessed Fixtures

410-68 Temperature

410-69 Enclosure

410-70 Lamp Wattage Marking

410-71 Solder Prohibited

410-72 Lampholders

Q. Special Provisions for Electric-Discharge Lighting Systems of 1000 Volts or Less

410-73 General

410-74 Direct-Current Equipment

410-75 Voltages—Dwelling Occupancies

410-76 Fixture Mounting

410-77 Equipment Not Integral with Fixture

410-78 Autotransformers

410-79 Switches

R. Special Provisions for Electric-Discharge Lighting Systems of More Than 1000 Volts

410-80 General

410-81 Control

410-82 Lamp Terminals and Lampholders

410-83 Transformer Ratings

410-84 Transformer Type

410-85 Transformer Secondary Connections

410-86 Transformer Locations

410-87 Transformer Loading

410-88 Wiring Method—Secondary Conductors

410-89 Lamp Supports

410-90 Exposure to Damage

410-91 Marking

410-92 Snap Switches

S. Lighting Track

410-100 Definition

410-101 Installation

410-102 Track Load

410-103 Heavy-Duty Track

410-104 Fastening

410-105 Construction Requirements

ARTICLE 422
APPLIANCES

A. General

422-1 Scope

This covers electric appliances used in any type of occupancy.

422-2 Live Parts

No live parts can be normally exposed. An exception to this is in toasters, grills, and the like when current-carrying parts must be exposed at high temperatures.

422-3 Other Articles

All other parts of the Code apply when applicable. When used in hazardous areas, Articles 500 through 517 apply. Article 430 applies to motor appliances and Article 440 applies to appliances with hermetic refrigerant motors.

B. Branch-Circuit Requirements

422-5 Branch-Circuit Sizing

Generally, the rating of the circuit must be at least that of the total rating of the appliance for an individual appliance branch circuit. There are three exceptions. Motor circuits are rated higher in accordance with Part B of Article 430. If the appliance is to be operated continuously (not a motor), the branch circuit must be rated at least 125% of the appliance unless the branch-circuit device and assembly are rated for continuous loading at 100%, in which case the branch circuit cannot be less than 100% of the appliance. Branch circuits for household cooking appliances are to be rated as provided in Table 220-19. If the branch circuit supplies an appliance and other loads, use the provisions of Section 210-23.

422-6 Branch-Circuit Overcurrent Protection

Must be protected in accordance with Section 240-3. If a protective device rating is marked on an appliance, this rating must not be exceeded.

C. Installation of Appliances

422-7 General

422-8 Flexible Cords

Specific types of cords are indicated for specific uses.

422-9 Cord- and Plug-Connected Immersion Heaters

422-10 Protection of Combustible Materials

422-11 Stands for Cord- and Plug-Connected Appliances

422-12 Signals for Heated Appliances

422-13 Flatirons

422-14 Water Heaters

422-15 Infrared Lamp Industrial Heating Appliances

422-16 Grounding

422-17 Wall-Mounted Ovens and Counter-Mounted Cooking Units

These appliances can be installed with a plug and receptacle combination only for ease in servicing or installation. If a plug and receptacle is used, it is not to be considered the disconnecting means required and they must be approved for the temperature in the space.

422-18 Support of Ceiling Fans

422-19 Other Installation Methods

D. Control and Protection of Appliances

422-20 Disconnecting Means

This must be provided as described in this part. If supplied by more than one source, all disconnects must be grouped.

422-21 Disconnection of Permanently Connected Appliances

If the device is not over 300 V A or ⅛ hp, the branch-circuit overcurrent device can be the disconnecting means. If the ratings are higher, the branch-circuit overcurrent device can only be used as the disconnecting means if it is accessible to the user. An exception is made for an appliance with a unit switch as permitted in Section 422-24.

422-22 Disconnection of Cord- and Plug-Connected Appliances

For these types of appliances an accessible separable connector or plug and receptacle can be used as the disconnecting means. In the case of the household range, the plug and receptacle must be accessible from the front either directly or through removal of a drawer. The receptacle or connector must be rated at least the same as the appliance. Demand factors are permitted if authorized in other sections of the *NEC®*. The attachment plugs and connectors must be constructed so that live parts cannot be inadvertently touched; if a single-pole switching device is used, the plug must be the grounding type and polarized, and designed so as to be able to interrupt the rated current and not to fit into a receptacle of lesser rating.

422-24 Unit Switch(es) as Disconnecting Means

A unit switch or switches that is part of the appliance can be considered the disconnecting means for the appliance if it has a position marked "off," disconnects all ungrounded conductors and other disconnecting means are installed as follows:

(a) In multifamily dwellings this other disconnecting means must be installed at least on the same floor that the appliance is installed. It can control other appliances and lamps.

(b) In two-family dwellings this other disconnecting means can be installed outside the dwelling unit and it can be a switch for the dwelling unit, such as in a panel in the basement.

(c) The service disconnect will fulfill this other requirement in a one-family dwelling.

(d) In all other occupancies, if readily accessible, the branch unit switch or circuit breaker can be used as the other disconnecting means.

422-25 Switch and Circuit Breaker to Be Indicating

422-26 Disconnecting Means for Motor-Driven Appliances

In the case of a permanently installed motor-driven appliance that is larger than ⅛ hp, a switch or circuit breaker can be used if it is in sight of the appliance. It does not have to be in sight if it is the other disconnecting means, as noted in Section 422-24.

422-27 Overcurrent Protection

(a) Appliances. They are permitted to be protected when they have branch circuits as indicated in Sections 422-5 and 422-6 and paragraphs (b) and (f) in this section. Motors are excepted and must comply with Articles 430 and 440 where applicable.

(b) Household-Type Appliance with Surface Heating Elements. If its demand is more than 60 A when calculated with Table 220-19, it must have its power supply subdivided with no circuit more than 50 A.

(c) Infrared Lamp Commercial and Industrial Heating Appliances. Cannot be greater than 50 A.

(d) Open-Coil or Exposed Sheathed-Coil Types of Surface Heating Elements in Commercial-Type Heating Appliances. Cannot be greater than 50 A.

(e) Single Nonmotor-Operated Appliance. The branch-circuit overcurrent device rating should not exceed the protective device rating noted on the unit. If no rating is noted, use 20 A if the unit rating is not more than 13.3 A and 150% of unit rating if more than 13.3 A.

(f) Electric Heating Appliances Employing Resistance-Type Heating Elements Rated More Than 48 Amperes. Factory-installed overcurrent devices which must be used in this case are discussed in this paragraph.

E. Marking of Appliances

422-30 Nameplate

An easily accessible or visible nameplate with a name and rating in volts and amperes or volts and watts must be installed. Frequency must be noted when applicable.

422-31 Marking of Heating Elements

They must be marked if rated over 1 A, are replaceable in the field, and are part of an appliance.

422-32 Appliances Consisting of Motors and Other Loads

ARTICLE 424 FIXED ELECTRIC SPACE HEATING EQUIPMENT

A. General

424-1 Scope

This article does not apply to heating and room air conditioning. It does apply to heating cables, unit boilers, central systems, and other fixed electric space heating equipment.

424-2 Other Articles

All applicable rules of the *NEC*® apply.

424-3 Branch Circuits

(a) Branch-Circuit Requirements. It can be any size as long as it is an individual branch circuit supplying only one appliance. If more than one appliance is on the circuit, 30 A is the largest rating permitted (50 A for nonresidential infrared heating equipment).

(b) Branch-Circuit Sizing. Generally, the branch-circuit size and overcurrent rating must be at least 125% of the rating of the appliance. There are a few exceptions. These include contactors and relays [refer to Section 210-22(c) Exception No. 2], and fixed electric space heating equipment, including hermetic refrigeration equipment (refer to Sections 440-34 and 440-35).

B. Installation

424-9 General

424-10 Special Permission

424-11 Supply Conductors

424-12 Locations

This equipment cannot be installed where it may be severely damaged unless protected. When installed in damp or wet locations, the equipment has to be approved for such locations.

424-13 Spacing from Combustible Materials

Adequate spacing must be provided unless approved for direct contact.

424-14 Grounding

Exposed metal parts which will probably become energized must be grounded in accordance with Article 250.

C. Control and Protection of Fixed Electric Space Heating Equipment

424-19 Disconnecting Means

This must be provided. When more than one source is used, all disconnecting means must be grouped.

(a) Heating Equipment with Supplementary Overcurrent Protection. Must be in sight of and on the supply side of the overcurrent device in addition to item 1 or 2 following.

1. *Heater Containing No Motor Rated Over 1/8 Horsepower.* This disconnecting means or

a unit switch complying with Section 424-19(c) can be used as the disconnecting means for the motor controller and heater if it is in sight of the motor controller and heater or can be locked in the open position.

2. *Heater Containing a Motor(s) Rated Over 1/8 Horsepower.* The same holds true as noted in the preceding subparagraph (1). In addition, if it is not in sight of the heater, a separate disconnect complying with Section 424-19(c) can be installed. If it is not in sight of the motor controller location, a disconnect means must be installed in accordance with Section 430-102, and where the motor is not in sight of the controller must comply with Section 430-102(b).

(b) Heating Equipment without Supplementary Overcurrent Protection

1. *Without Motor or with Motor Not Over 1/8 Horsepower.* The branch-circuit switch or circuit breaker can serve as the disconnecting means.
2. *Over 1/8 Horsepower.* A disconnecting means must be located within sight of the motor controller except when installed in accordance with Section 424-19(a)(2).

(c) Unit Switches as Disconnecting Means. A unit switch that is part of the heater disconnects all ungrounded conductors and has a marked off position can be used as the disconnecting means if other disconnecting means are installed as follows:

1. In multifamily family dwellings, this disconnecting means must be installed at least on the same floor as the heater. It can control other heaters and lamps.

2. In two-family dwellings this disconnecting means can be installed either inside or outside the dwelling unit. There is also a provision for additional control.

3. In one-family dwellings the service disconnect can serve this purpose.

4. In other occupancies, if readily accessible, the branch-circuit switch or circuit breaker can be used.

424-20 Thermostatically Controlled Switching Devices

These devices can also serve as the disconnecting means if all the following conditions are met; have a marked off position, interrupt all ungrounded conductors when manually put in that position, cannot be automatically energized in the off position, and are located in accordance with Section 424-19.

424-21 Switch and Circuit Breaker to Be Indicating

424-22 Overcurrent Protection

Branch-circuit protection as provided in Article 210 can be used. Motors must comply with Articles 430 and 440. Resistance element cannot be protected at a higher rating than 60 A. Equipment rated at more than 48 A must be subdivided, with each subdivision rated not more than 48 A. The manufacturers must provide the division and overcurrent protection for the division.

Field conductors between the heater and supplementary overcurrent protection must be sized at 125% of the load if the heater is rated less than 50 kW.

If the heater is rated at least 50 kW the conductors can be sized at 100% of the rating if the heater is marked for 100% conductor rating and the conductors are not smaller than the marked rating. Also, a temperature control device must be installed.

D. Marking of Heating Equipment

424-28 Nameplate

Must have proper marking information: volts, amperes, horsepower, etc.

424-29 Marking of Heating Elements

Volts and amperes or volts and watts.

E. Electric Space Heating Cables

424-34 Heating Cable Construction

Nonheating cables of at least 7 ft must be installed at the factory.

424-35 Marking of Heating Cables

Proper marking is required. Special color coding is required for different voltages of heating cables: 120 V, yellow; 208 V, blue; 240 V, red; 277 V, brown.

424-36 Clearances of Wiring in Ceilings

Two inches of space is required above a heated ceiling. An operating ambient temperature of 50°C is to be used for all sizing. If located above thermal insulation 2 in. in thickness, the temperature correction is not needed.

424-37 Location of Branch-Circuit and Feeder Wiring in Walls

Comply with Article 300 and Section 310-10.

424-38 Area Restrictions

The cables cannot go beyond the room in which they originate. They cannot be installed in closets or over a partition that extends to the ceiling. There is also a restriction as to how they may be run over cabinets. They may be used in closet ceilings for low-temperature sources for humidity control, if there are no obstructions between floor and ceiling in that part of the ceiling.

424-39 Clearance from Other Objects and Openings

The heating cables must be at least 8 in. from boxes used for surface-mounted lighting fixtures and 2 in. from recessed lighting fixtures. They cannot be installed where they are covered by any surface mounted unit.

424-40 Splices

The cable's length cannot be changed.

424-41 Installation of Heating Cables on Dry Board, in Plaster and on Concrete Ceilings

(a) Cables are not permitted in walls unless it is a single run to reach a dropped ceiling.

(b) A minimum spacing of 1½ in. is required for cables rated at 2¾ W per foot and under.

(c) Heating cables cannot be applied directly to metal surfaces. They can be only to fire-resistant surfaces. A coat of plaster must be applied to a metal surface.

(d) The entire heating cable, at least 3 in. of the nonheating cable and the splice between them must be embedded in plaster or dry board.

(e) The surface of the ceiling must have a coating of at least ½ in. of plaster or other approved material.

(f) Cables have to be secured at a maximum of 16 in. on center unless approved for 6 in. on center.

(g) When dry board is used for the ceiling, it cannot be thicker than ½ in.

(h) Cables cannot come in contact with metal surfaces.

(i) The cables must be installed parallel to joists in a dry board installation and at least 2½ in. between center of adjacent runs of cable under the center line of the joist. Care must be taken not to drive nails through the heating cables.

424-42 Finished Ceilings

Coverings cannot have thermal insulating properties. Paint and wallpaper can be used.

424-43 Installation of Nonheating Leads of Cables and Panels

424-44 Installation of Cables in Concrete or Poured Masonry Floors

424-45 Inspection and Tests

F. Duct Heaters

424-57 General

424-58 Identification

424-59 Airflow

424-60 Elevated Inlet Temperature

Duct heaters must be approved for mounting in ducts and at the expected temperatures, as well as assure proper airflow.

424-61 Installation of Duct Heaters with Heat Pumps and Air Conditioning

424-62 Condensation

424-63 Fan Circuit Interlock

424-64 Limit Controls

424-65 Location of Disconnecting Means

Must be within sight of the controller except as noted in Section 424-19(a).

424-66 Installation

G. Resistance-Type Boilers

424-70 Scope

424-71 Identification

424-72 Overcurrent Protection

424-73 Over-Temperature Limit Control

424-74 Over-Pressure Limit Control

424-75 Grounding

H. Electrode-Type Boilers

424-80 Scope

424-81 Identification

424-82 Branch-Circuit Requirements

424-83 Over-Temperature Limit Control

424-84 Over-Pressure Limit Control

424-85 Grounding

424-86 Markings

I. Electric Radiant Heating Panels and Heating Panel Sets

424-90 Scope

424-91 Definition

424-92 Markings

424-93 Installation

424-94 Clearances of Wiring in Ceilings

424-95 Location of Branch-Circuit and Feeder Wiring in Walls

424-96 Connection to Branch-Circuit Conductors

424-97 Nonheating Leads

424-98 Installation in Poured Concrete or Poured Masonry

424-99 Installation under Floor Covering

ARTICLE 426
FIXED OUTDOOR ELECTRIC DE-ICING AND SNOW-MELTING EQUIPMENT

A. General

426-1 Scope

This article covers installations both embedded and exposed.

426-2 Definitions

426-3 Application of Other Articles

The rest of the *NEC*® is applicable unless changed by this article.

426-4 Branch-Circuit Sizing

Conductors and overcurrent protection must be at least 125% of the load. Exception 1 of Section 240-3 is permitted.

B. Installation

426-10 General

426-11 Use

426-12 Thermal Protection

Must be protected against contact by persons if operated at temperatures above 140°F.

426-13 Identification

Warning signs must be posted where used.

426-14 Special Permission

C. Resistance Heating Elements

426-20 Embedded De-icing and Snow-Melting Equipment

Units cannot exceed 120 W per square foot and must have at least 1 in. between cables. They can be installed either on an asphalt or masonry base at least 2 in. thick and covered with at least 1½ in. of asphalt or masonry, or on any approved type of base embedded in 3½ in. of asphalt or masonry and covered with at least 1½ in. of asphalt or masonry. They must be secured and not installed over bridge expansion joints unless proper provisions are made.

426-21 Exposed De-icing and Snow-Melting Equipment

They must be secured, proper temperature limiting, and have no cross-bridge expansion joints unless provided for.

426-22 Installation of Nonheating Leads for Embedded Equipment

426-23 Installation of Nonheating Leads for Exposed Equipment

426-24 Electrical Connection

426-25 Marking

426-26 Corrosion Protection

426-27 Grounding

D. Impedance Heating

426-30 Personnel Protection

426-31 Voltage Limitations

Must not operate at greater than 30 V ac. If ground fault circuit interrupter is used—80 V ac.

426-32 Isolation Transformer

426-33 Induced Currents

426-34 Grounding

E. Skin Effect Heating

426-40 Conductor Ampacity

426-41 Pull Boxes

426-42 Single Conductor in Enclosure

426-43 Corrosion Protection

426-44 Grounding

F. Control and Protection

426-50 Disconnecting Means

Must have a disconnecting means that opens all ungrounded wires. The branch-circuit breaker can be used if readily accessible. Also permitted is a factory installed attachment plug if it is rated not more than 20 A and 150 V to ground.

426-51 Controllers

If the temperature controller operates line current and has an off position, it must open all ungrounded conductors. It cannot be used as a disconnecting means unless it can be locked in the open position. If no off position is provided, it does not have to open all ungrounded conductors and cannot be used as a disconnecting means. If it controls a relay, it does not have to open all ungrounded conductors and cannot be used as a disconnecting means. There are also rules in the *NEC®* for combined switching devices.

426-52 Overcurrent Protection

Refer to Section 426-4.

ARTICLE 427 FIXED ELECTRIC HEATING EQUIPMENT FOR PIPELINES AND VESSELS

A. General

427-1 Scope

427-2 Definitions

427-3 Application of Other Articles

427-4 Branch-Circuit Sizing

B. Installation

427-10 General

427-11 Use

427-12 Thermal Protection

427-13 Identification

C. Resistance Heating Elements

427-14 Secured

427-15 Not in Direct Contact

427-16 Expansion and Contraction

427-17 Flexural Capability

427-18 Power Supply Leads

427-19 Electrical Connections

427-20 Marking

427-21 Grounding

427-22 Equipment Protection

D. Impedance Heating

427-25 Personnel Protection

427-26 Voltage Limitations

427-27 Isolation Transformer

427-28 Induced Currents

427-29 Grounding

427-30 Secondary Conductor Sizing

E. Induction Heating

427-35 Scope

427-36 Personnel Protection

427-37 Induced Current

F. Skin Effect Heating

427-45 Conductor Ampacity

427-46 Pull Boxes

427-47 Single Conductor Enclosure

427-48 Grounding

G. Control and Protection

427-55 Disconnecting Means

427-56 Controls

427-57 Overcurrent Protection

ARTICLE 430
MOTORS, MOTOR CIRCUITS, AND CONTROLLERS

A. General

430-1 Motor Feeder and Branch Circuits

This article covers requirements for motors, motor circuits, and controllers. Diagram 430-1 on page 70-355 of the *NEC*® describes where in Article 430 different parts of the circuits are covered as well as other articles. This article does not cover air-conditioning and refrigeration equipment, which is covered in Article 440.

430-2 Adjustable-Speed Drive Systems

430-3 Part Winding Motors

430-5 Other Articles

There are numerous other articles with which motor and controllers must comply for special cases.

430-6 Ampacity and Motor Rating Determination

Generally, Tables 310-16 through 310-19 are to be used for conductor selection and Tables 430-147 through 430-150 are used to determine ampere rating for sizes of wire switches, circuit protection, and the like (not the nameplate ratings). They are not used for separate motor overload protection. For this, the nameplate ratings are used. Exceptions to this rule are multispeed motors, shaded pole motors, permanent-split-capacitor-type fan or blower motors, torque motors, and ac adjustable voltage motors.

430-7 Marking on Motors and Multimotor Equipment

430-8 Marking on Controllers

430-9 Marking at Terminals

430-10 Wiring Space in Enclosures

Table 430-10(b) indicates the minimum wire bending space at the terminals of enclosed motors.

430-11 Protection against Liquids

430-12 Motor Terminal Housings

Tables 430-12(b), 430-12(c)(1), and 430-12(c)(2) give various dimension and space requirements.

430-13 Bushing

430-14 Location of Motors

430-16 Exposure to Dust Accumulations

430-17 Highest Rated (Largest) Motor

If this is to be determined, use the one with the largest rated full-load current.

430-18 Nominal Voltage of Rectifier Systems

B. Motor Circuit Conductors

430-21 General

The rules of this section apply to circuits supplying motors at 600 V or less. Section 430-124 applies to motors over 600 V.

430-22 Single Motor

Generally size conductors at 125% of the motor full-load rated current for the supply to a single motor (use Tables 430-147 through 430-150). There are two exceptions to this rule. The first is for short-time intermittent, periodic, or varying duty. For these, use the values in Table 430-22(a). The second is for direct-current motors that operate from a single-phase power supply which is rectified.

When the junction box is allowed to be separated from the motor, a special exception is made for wire size on motors of 1 hp or less.

430-23 Wound-Rotor Secondary

The secondary leads for a continuous-duty wound-rotor motor must be rated at least 125% of the full-load secondary current. If the motor is not continuous, Table 430-22(a) must be used. Table 430-23(c) is used when the secondary resistor is separate from the controller.

430-24 Conductors Supplying Several Motors

In this case the conductors are rated at 125% of the full-load current of the largest motor (the same as a single motor) plus the full-load current of all additional motors. In the case of a mixture of continuous and noncontinuous duty motors, find the largest rated motor using Table 430-22(a) and 100% for a continuous-duty motor. Add their ratings together plus an additional 25% for the largest rating.

430-25 Conductors Supplying Motors and Other Loads

The rating of the conductors must be the total of all loads as calculated by the respective applicable sections of the *NEC*®.

430-26 Feeder Demand Factor

If all motors will not operate simultaneously for any number of reasons, the authority having jurisdiction can allow the use of a demand factor.

430-27 Capacitors with Motors

430-28 Feeder Taps

Feeder tap conductors can be smaller than the feeder under a number of rules. They must be sized at least according to Part B of this section and either be enclosed and 10 ft or less in length or be one-third or more of the rating of the feeder, 25 ft or less in length, and protected. There is an exception for feeder taps over 25 feet in high bay manufacturing buildings.

430-29 Constant Voltage DC Motors-Power Resistors

C. Motor and Branch-Circuit Overload Protection

430-31 General

The overload protection is usually the thermal overloads in the controller or starter. It should not be confused with the short-circuit protection, which is the fuse or circuit breaker in the panelboard (Diagram 430-1 in the Code should be referred to), as well as example 8, Chapter 9.

430-32 Continuous-Duty Motors

There are four methods acceptable:

(a) More Than 1 Horsepower

1. A separate overload device must be used. It must be rated at not more than 125% of the motor nameplate rating if the motor is rated with a temperature rise of not more than 40°C or a service factor of 1.15 or more. The rating is reduced to 115% for all other motors. Exceptions are provided in Section 430-34.
2. Thermal protectors as part of the motor are listed in this paragraph.
3. If the motor is part of an approved assembly, will not normally have overloads, and has some protection against failure to start, additional overload protection is not necessary.
4. Motors larger than 1500 hp are discussed in this paragraph.

(b) One Horsepower or Less, Nonautomatically Started. If it is within sight of the controller location, the ground-fault protection and branch-circuit short-circuit protection is sufficient. The sizings noted in Part D are to be used. It can be on a 120-V circuit rated 20 A or less. If not within sight of the controller or permanently installed, it must comply with Section 430-32(c), which follows.

(c) One Horsepower or Less, Automatically Started. Here again there are four acceptable methods; the first three are similar to the first three for motors rated more than 1 hp. These include separate devices (ratings are indicated), thermal protectors, and cases where no additional protection other than branch-circuit protection is required. A fourth case is that where the impedance of the motor protects against overheating when the motor does not start.

(d) Wound-Rotor Secondaries. These can have a motor overload device.

430-33 Intermittent and Similar Duty

You can omit the separate overload protection for these types of motors and use only the branch-circuit short-circuit and ground-fault protective device.

430-34 Selection of Overload Relay

In the event the ratings chosen as listed in Section 430-32(a)(1) and (c)(1) will not allow the motor to start, this section gives larger permissible ratings.

430-35 Shunting during Starting Period

There are cases where the overload protection can be shunted during starting.

430-36 Fuses—in Which Conductor

When used as overload protection, put one in each ungrounded conductor and also the grounded conductor if the supply is three-phase, three-wire ac with one phase grounded.

430-37 Devices Other Than Fuses—in Which Conductor

Table 430-37 gives the requirements.

430-38 Number of Conductors Opened by Overload Devices

The number of conductors to be opened must prevent current to the motor for devices other than fuses, thermal cutouts, or thermal protection.

430-39 Motor Controller as Overload Protection

This is permitted if it is in accordance with Table 430-37 and operator in the running position and also in the starting position for an ac motor.

430-40 Thermal Cutouts and Overload Relays

If the device used for motor overload protection cannot clear short circuits, they must be protected by either fuses or circuit breakers or a motor short-circuit protector sized as noted in Section 430-52. There are two exceptions to the sizing rule—group installations and where a thermal cutout or overload relay is used—both where approved and the rating is marked in the equipment.

430-42 Motors on General-Purpose Branch Circuits

This section indicates what overload protection must be used when motors are connected to general-purpose branch circuits. It must also comply with Article 210.

(a) Not Over 1 Horsepower. Can be connected without overload protection if the rules of Section 430-32(b) and (c) and Section 430-53(a)(1) and (a)(2) are followed.

(b) Over 1 Horsepower. Each motor must have overload protection as noted in Section 430-32.

(c) Cord- and Plug-Connected. If no overload protection is provided, as in (a) above, the ratings of the plug and receptacle cannot be larger than 15 A 125 V or 10 A 250 V. If protection is provided as in (b) above, the overload device must be part of the motor or appliance.

(d) Time Delay. Time delay must be provided in the branch-circuit and ground-fault devices to let the motor start.

430-43 Automatic Restarting

430-44 Orderly Shutdown

If an orderly shutdown is necessary to protect people rather than a quick opening of the circuit, the overload device can be connected to an alarm rather than open the circuit under the provisions of this section.

D. Motor Branch-Circuit, Short-Circuit, and Ground-Fault Protection

430-51 General

430-52 Rating or Setting for Individual Motor Circuit

The device must carry the starting current. Table 430-152 lists the maximum settings. If the values in the tables are not a standard-size device, the rating can be increased to the next highest rating. If the rating in the table will not permit the motor to start, the rating can be increased as follows:

1. Nontime delay fuse less than 601 A up to 400% of full-load current
2. Time delay fuses up to 225% of full-load current
3. Circuit breakers (inverse time) up to 400% for full-load currents of up to 100 A and 300% for larger currents
4. Fuses between 601 and 6000 A up to 300% of full-load current

An exception is provided for torque motor branch circuits. Also listed in this section are the rules for when instantaneous trip circuit breakers and motor short-circuit protectors can be used. Also, rules are indicated for multispeed motors. Where a maximum rating is indicated by the manufacturer, it cannot be exceeded.

430-53 Several Motors or Loads on One Branch Circuit

This section indicates under what conditions two or more motors or combined loads are permitted on one branch circuit.

(a) If none of the motors is greater than 1 hp, the circuit is protected at 20 A at 120 V or not more than 15 A at 600 V, the full-load current of each motor is not more than 6 A, individual overload protection meets the requirements of Section 430-32, and the rating marked on any controller for branch-circuit short circuit and ground-fault protection is not exceeded, more than one motor or combination loads are permitted on one branch circuit.

(b) When the branch-circuit short circuit and ground-fault protective devices rating is not larger than required for the smallest motor and all motors have individual overload protection and the combination load will operate under these conditions, more than one motor or combination loads are permitted.

(c) Group installations of more than one motor or combination loads are permitted if the overload devices and motor controllers are in a listed factory assembly, and motor short circuit and ground-fault protection are in the assembly or noted on the assembly; or if the controllers, overload devices, branch circuit, short circuit, and ground-fault devices are field-installed separately with manufacturer's instructions for use with each other and the following conditions are met:

1. The overload device must be approved for group installation and have a specified maximum fuse or inverse time circuit breaker rating.
2. The motor controller for each motor must comply with the same rules as in (1) above.
3. The circuit breakers must be approved for group installation and have inverse time characteristics.
4. The rating of the fuse or circuit breaker for the branch circuit must comply with rules of Sections 430-52 and 240-3, Exception 1. It must be at least that of Section 430-52 for the largest motor and the sum of full-load ratings of other motors and loads.
5. The rating allowed in Section 430-40 for the smallest motor will also be the maximum for the branch-circuit fuses or inverse time circuit breakers.

(d) In a group installation as described in (c) above, if the conductors to any single motor are not larger than the branch-circuit conductors or are not less than one-third the rating of the branch-circuit conductors in accordance with Section 430-22, and not farther than 25 ft from the controller and physically protected, then installation will not require individual branch-circuit short-circuit and ground-fault protection.

430-54 Multimotor and Combination-Load Equipment

The branch-circuit short-circuit and ground-fault device rating must not be larger than the rating marked on the equipment and comply with Section 430-7(d).

430-55 Combined Overcurrent Protection

As long as the rating is not larger than that required for overload protection in Section 430-32, the branch-circuit short-circuit and ground-fault protection and overload protection can be in one device.

430-56 Branch-Circuit Protective Devices—in Which Conductor

430-57 Size of Fuseholder

430-58 Rating of Circuit Breaker

E. Motor Feeder Short-Circuit and Ground-Fault Protection

430-61 General

430-62 Rating or Setting—Motor Load

The rating must be that of the largest branch-circuit protective device plus the full-load currents of all other motors. If larger feeders have been installed for future expansion, the rating can be that of the feeder. Reference is made to Sections 430-24 and 440-22(a) and Table 430-152.

430-63 Rating or Setting—Power and Light Loads

When combined loads are installed in one feeder, the rating can be the combination of that permitted by Articles 210 and 220 for lighting and appliances plus that permitted by Section 430-52 for a single motor and Section 430-62 for more than one motor.

F. Motor Control Circuits

430-71 General

The motor control circuit carries the electric signal to control the controller but not power for the circuit.

430-72 Overcurrent Protection

If the circuit is tapped from the load side of a branch-circuit protective device, it must have protection as specified in Section 430-72. If not, it must be protected as specified in Section 725-12 or 725-35. Values for overcurrent protection for conductors are specified in Table 430-72(b). There are four exceptions to this rule.

There are also requirements for a control circuit transformer.

430-73 Mechanical Protection of Conductor

430-74 Disconnection

Motor control circuits must have a disconnecting means. One device can disconnect both the motor and control circuits from power, or separate ones can be used. If a transformer is used, the disconnecting means must be in the supply side of the transformer.

G. Motor Controllers

430-81 General

The word "controller" is defined in Article 100. Here it can mean a device or switch to stop and start a motor by breaking the motor circuit current. When the motor is stationary and of not more than ⅛ hp, the branch-circuit protective device can be used if the motor is normally left running and cannot be damaged by not starting or by overloads. The plug and receptacle can be the controller if the motor is portable and not more than ⅓ hp.

430-82 Controller Design

430-83 Rating

Generally, it must have a horsepower rating at least equal to that of the motor. There are three exceptions: for motors of not more than 2 hp, for use as a branch-circuit breaker, and for a torque motor.

430-84 Need Not Open All Conductors

Unless it serves as a disconnecting device, it does not have to open all conductors.

430-85 In Grounded Conductors

This is permitted if it also simultaneously opens all other conductors.

430-87 Number of Motors Served by Each Controller

Each motor must normally have its own controller. There are exceptions to this rule if the motors are rated at not more than 600 V and the single controller is rated at not less than the sum of all motors it will control. Under these conditions it is allowed if more than one motor is used in one device or one overcurrent device is used for a group of motors [Section 430-53(a)] or the motors are in one room in sight of the controller.

430-88 Adjustable-Speed Motors

430-89 Speed Limitation

430-90 Combination Fuseholder and Switch as Controller

430-91 Motor Controller Enclosure Types

H. Disconnecting Means

430-101 General

430-102 Location

It must be in sight from the controller location. An exception is made for motors over 600 V if it can be locked out and a warning sign is posted. Also, one disconnect can be used for a group of controllers for a multimotor device. A disconnecting means must also be located within sight of the motor location except in accordance with Section 430-102(a).

430-103 To Disconnect Both Motor and Controller

430-104 To Be Indicating

430-105 Grounded Conductors

If all conductors are opened simultaneously, one pole can be in a grounded conductor.

430-106 Service Switch as Disconnecting Means

If one motor is the entire installation, the service switch can be the disconnect device if it meets the requirements of Article 430.

430-107 Readily Accessible

430-108 Every Switch

430-109 Type

Generally, it must be a horsepower-rated motor circuit switch or a circuit breaker. There are six exceptions.

Exception No. 1. The branch-circuit overcurrent device can be used for stationary motors of 1/8 hp or less.

Exception No. 2. Stationary motors 2 hp or less and 300 V or less can have a general-use switch rated twice that of the motor. A general-use snap switch (ac only) can be used on ac circuits if the motor is not more than 80% of the rating of the switch.

Exception No. 3. Motors over 2 hp up to 100 hp. A general-use switch can be used for autotransformer controllers if the motor drives a generator with overload protection; the controller can interrupt locked rotor current, has no voltage release, and has running overload protection not larger than 125% of full-load current; separate fuses or inverse time circuit breakers are provided and rated not more than 150% of full-load current.

Exception No. 4. Stationary motors more than 40 hp dc or 100 hp ac can have a general use or isolating switch if marked "Do Not Operate Under Load."

Exception No. 5. Cord- and plug-connected motors can use horsepower-rated attachment plugs and receptacles rated at least that of the motor. This is not required for cord and plug appliances (Section 422-22) and room air conditioners (Section 440-63).

Exception No. 6. A general-use switch can be used for a torque motor.

430-110 Ampere Rating and Interrupting Capacity

(a) It must have a rating of at least 115% of the full-load current rating of the motor.

(b) It must have a rating of at least 115% of the nameplate current for torque motors.

(c) For combination loads of motors or motors and other types of loads, the ratings of the disconnect must not be less than 115% of the total of the full-load current of all the loads.

430-111 Switch or Circuit Breaker as Both Controller and Disconnecting Means

A switch or circuit breaker can be used as the disconnect and controller if it complies with Section 430-83: if it opens all ungrounded conductors to the motor, has an overcurrent protective device which opens all ungrounded conductors to the switch, an inverse time circuit breaker, or an oil switch.

430-112 Motors Served by Single Disconnecting Means

Generally, a motor must have its own disconnecting means. There is an exception.

430-113 Energy from More Than One Source

Generally, each source must have a disconnect. There are two exceptions.

J. Over 600 Volts, Nominal

430-121 General

430-122 Marking on Controllers

430-123 Conductor Enclosures Adjacent to Motors

430-124 Size of Conductors

430-125 Motor Circuit Overload Protection

430-126 Rating of Motor Control Apparatus

430-127 Disconnecting Means

K. Protection of Live Parts—All Voltages

430-131 General

430-132 Where Required

If operating at 50 V or more, the exposed live parts must be guarded against accidental contact by enclosure or location. This can be done in a special room or enclosure, on a balcony or by installation at least 8 ft above the floor.

430-133 Guards for Attendants

If the only guards are by location, as noted in Section 430-132, then insulating mats or platforms are required.

L. Grounding All Voltages

430-141 General

430-142 Stationary Motors

The frames must be grounded if in a wet location and not isolated, supplied by wire in a metal enclosure, in a hazardous location, or if motor operates over 150 V to ground.

430-143 Portable Motors

430-144 Controllers

430-145 Method of Grounding

ARTICLE 440
AIR CONDITIONING
AND REFRIGERATING EQUIPMENT

A. General

440-1 Scope

This section states the scope.

440-2 Definitions

440-3 Other Articles

Many additional articles are listed, such as 422, 424, 430, 460, and 470, and some not in Chapter 4.

440-4 Marking on Hermetic Refrigerant Motor-Compressors and Equipment

440-5 Marking on Controllers

440-6 Ampacity and Rating

The rating on the nameplate is to be used for a hermetic refrigerant motor compressor. Conductors are to be chosen from Tables 310-16 through 310-31.

440-7 Highest Rated (Largest) Motor

440-8 Single Machine

A refrigerating system or air-conditioning system can be considered in accordance with Section 430-87, exception, and Section 430-112, exception.

B. Disconnecting Means

440-11 General

440-12 Rating and Interrupting Capacity

It must be at least 115% of the larger of the rated load or branch-circuit selection circuit. If this rating comes out to be 100 hp or larger, use the provisions of Section 430-109, Exception No. 4. Additional information is given concerning equivalent horsepower, combination loads, small motor compressors and switches.

440-13 Cord-Connected Equipment

The separable connector or plug and receptacle can be used as the disconnecting means.

440-14 Location

It must be within sight and readily accessible to the equipment.

C. Branch-Circuit Short-Circuit and Ground-Fault Protection

440-21 General

440-22 Application and Selection

(a) Rating or Setting for Individual Motor-Compressor. It must allow the motor to start. The *NEC®* therefore permits a rating or setting of up to 175% of the larger of the motor load or branch-circuit selection current. This can be increased to 225% if necessary. A 15 ampere rating is the least that can be required for branch-circuit short-circuit and ground-fault protection.

(b) Rating or Setting for Equipment. It must also allow the equipment to start. If only one hermetic refrigerant motor compressor is used, conform to Section 422(a). If more than one hermetic refrigerant motor compressor is used, conform to Section 430-53 and the following:

1. If the hermetic refrigerant motor compressor is the largest load, use Section 440-22(a) for this plus the other loads.
2. If the hermetic refrigerant motor compressor is not the largest load, the sum is that of the rating of the motor compressor loads plus the value noted in Section 430-53(c)(4) or Section 240-3 for other loads, whichever is applicable. There are two exceptions. For a detailed analysis, refer to the *NEC®* and one of the many reference guides.

(c) If a maximum rating is indicated by the manufacturer, it should not be exceeded.

D. Branch-Circuit Conductors

440-31 General

440-32 Single Motor-Compressor

The rating cannot be less than 125% of the largest of the motor compressor rated load or branch-circuit selection current.

440-33 Motor-Compressor(s) with or without Additional Motor Loads

The ampacity must be the sum of the larger of the rated load or branch-circuit selection currents of all the motor-compressor loads plus full-load currents of the other motors plus 25% of the largest motor. There are two exceptions to this: one is for room air conditioners as per Part G and the other is for interlocked motors.

440-34 Combination Load

The capacity must be adequate for all other loads, plus the motor-compressor load as specified in Sections 430-32 and 440-33. An exception is also made for interlocked circuitry.

440-35 Multimotor and Combination-Load Equipment

It cannot be less than that marked on the equipment as per Section 440-3(b).

E. Controller for Motor-Compressor

440-41 Rating

Generally, use the nameplate ratings (refer to Sections 440-5 and 440-6). If more than one load is served, use the combined load rating [refer to Section 440-12(b)].

F. Motor Compressor and Branch-Circuit Overload Protection

440-51 General

440-52 Application and Selection

(a) Protection of Motor-Compressor. The following methods can be used: (1) an overload relay that will trip at not more than 140% of motor full-load current; (2) a thermal protector integral with the motor compressor; (3) a fuse or inverse time circuit breaker responsive to motor current and rated not more than 125% of motor current; and (4) a protective system furnished with the unit or specified for the unit.

(b) Protection of Motor-Compressor Control Apparatus and Branch-Circuit Conductors. The same types of devices used in Section 440-52(a) are permitted. It can be the same device protecting the motor-compressor in accordance with Section 440-52(a).

440-53 Overload Relays

440-54 Motor-Compressors and Equipment on 15 or 20 Ampere Branch Circuits—Not Cord and Attachment Plug-Connected

440-55 Cord and Attachment Plug-Connected Motor-Compressors and Equipment on 15 or 20 Ampere Branch Circuits

G. Provisions for Room Air Conditioners

440-60 General

440-61 Grounding

440-62 Branch-Circuit Requirements

The branch circuit can only have a load of 80% of its rating for a cord- and plug-connected air-conditioning unit, if no other loads are on the circuit. If other loads are on the circuit, then the load of the cord- and plug-connected air-conditioning unit cannot be more than 50% of the rating of the branch circuit.

440-63 Disconnecting Means

The attachment plug can be used for a single-phase unit at 250 Volts or less if the manual control on the unit is readily accessible and within 6 ft of the floor or if a manual switch is readily accessible within sight of the unit.

440-64 Supply Cords

The length of the cord cannot be larger than 10 ft for 120 V or 6 ft for 208 to 240 V.

The following article titles are listed for reference: **Article 445**—Generators; **Article 450**—Transformers and Transformer Vaults (Including Secondary Ties); **Article 460**—Capacitors; **Article 470**—Resistors and Reactors; **Article 480**—Storage Batteries.

5

SPECIAL OCCUPANCIES

ARTICLE 500 HAZARDOUS (CLASSIFIED) LOCATIONS

500-1 Scope—Articles 500 through 503

Articles 500 through 503 describe the electrical equipment and wiring requirements in locations where a fire or explosion hazard can exist because of flammable gases or vapors, flammable liquids, combustible dust, or ignitible fibers or flyings.

500-2 Location and General Requirements

The classifications are arrived at as a result of the items noted above and their properties. Intrinsically

Note: Space does not permit a complete description of this chapter. This is true of the entire *NEC*® but is again stated here. Only the highlights are noted. The reader should refer to the *NEC*® for complete descriptions.

safe items are permitted and are not governed by Articles 500 through 517. Additional explanatory fine-print notes are indicated.

500-3 Special Precaution

This section indicates the groupings of various air mixtures. Requirements are given for approval for class and properties, marking and temperature. Additional information is given in the form of fine print notes.

500-4 Specific Occupancies

These are covered in Articles 510 through 517 and include garages, aircraft hangars, gasoline dispensing and service stations, bulk storage plants, finishing processes, and health care facilities.

500-5 Class I Locations

Areas where flammable gases or vapors are in the air in quantities that can cause explosive or ignitible mixtures are classified as Class I. They are further broken down into two divisions:

(a) Class I, Division 1. This is where ignitible concentrations of gases or vapors can exist normally; where they may exist because of maintenance or leakage; or where they might exist because of breakdowns or faulty operations.

(b) Class I, Division 2. This is where volatile flammable liquids or flammable gases are used but are normally in closed containers or systems and can escape only as a result of a breakdown or rupture; where ignitible concentration of gases or vapors normally cannot occur because of mechanical ventilation; where an area is next to a Class I, Division 1, location and some leakage between areas occurs.

500-6 Class II Locations

These are hazardous because of combustible dust. They are also broken down into two divisions.

(a) Class II, Division 1. This is where combustible dust is in the air and can ignite under normal conditions due to its concentration, or where a breakdown of equipment can cause these concentrations and an ignitible source, or the dust may be electrically conductive in hazardous quantities.

(b) Class II, Division 2. This is where the concentrations of the dust are normally not high enough to ignite or explode and will not interfere with the operation of electrical equipment or other equipment; but can be in the air because of occasional breakdown of handling of processing equipment and can be ignited by electrical equipment or other equipment or prevent safe dissipation of heat from it.

500-7 Class III Locations

Areas that have ignitible fibers or flyings in a concentration not likely to cause ignition are classified as Class III. They are also further broken down into two divisions.

(a) Class III, Division 1. Areas where the fibers or flyings are handled, manufactured, or used.

(b) Class III, Division 2. Areas where the fibers or flyings are stored or handled. An exception is made in the process of manufacture.

ARTICLE 501
CLASS I LOCATIONS

501-1 General

This article refers to those areas classified as Class I.

501-2 Transformers and Capacitors

(a) Class I, Division 1

1. *Containing liquid that will burn.* They must be installed in an approved vault (Sections 450-41 through 450-48) with no door or opening

to the Class I, Division 1, locations, with proper ventilation and the vents going outside the buildings and being large enough to relieve an explosion. The ducts for the vents must be constructed of reinforced concrete.

2. *Not containing liquid that will burn*. These must be installed in a vault as noted in (a)(1) or be approved for a Class I location.

(b) Class I, Division 2. In these locations they must be in accordance with Sections 450-21 through 450-27.

501-3 Meters, Instruments, and Relays

(a) Class I, Division 1. They must be in Class I, Division 1, enclosures.

(b) Class I, Division 2

1. *Contacts*. Make-or-break contacts, switches, circuit breakers, etc., must have an approved Class I, Division 1, enclosure. Three exceptions are: immersed in oil, in a hermetically sealed chamber, or where insufficient energy is released to cause ignition.
2. *Resistors and similar equipment*. These must have an approved Class I, Division 1, enclosure. An exception is made if the exposed surface does not exceed 80% of the ignition temperature and there are no make-or-break or sliding contacts.
3. *Without make-or-break contacts*. General-purpose enclosures can be used for this category for transformer windings, impedence coils, solenoids, and other windings.
4. *General-purpose assemblies*. If an assembly has items that can use general-purpose enclosures [noted in (b)(1), (b)(2), and (b)(3)], a single, general-purpose enclosure can be used. If equipment noted in (b)(2) is used, the maximum surface temperature must be noted.
5. *Fuses*. Fuses for instrument circuits not sub-

ject to overloading can be mounted in general-purpose enclosures if approved in (b)(1) through (b)(4), and if they are preceded by a switch in accordance with (b)(1).

6. *Connections*. Process control can use a cord, plug, and receptacle if (a) an approved Class I, Division 1, switch is also used; (b) current is not greater than 3 A at 120 V; (c) cord is not longer than 3 ft, is rated for extra hard usage or hard usage depending on location, and uses locking and grounding-type plug and receptacle; and (d) a warning is posted against unplugging under load.

501-4 Wiring Methods

(a) Class I, Division 1. Only threaded rigid metal conduit, threaded steel intermediate conduit, cr Type MI cable can be used. Boxes and fittings must be explosion proof and joints threaded. At least five threads must be engaged.

(b) Class I, Division 2. Methods permitted are threaded rigid metal conduit; threaded steel intermediate metal conduit; enclosed gasketed busways; enclosed gasketed wireways; Type MI, MC, MV, TC or SNM cable with approved terminations; Type PLTC cable. Explosion proof boxes or fittings are not required. Additional requirements are noted.

501-5 Sealing and Drainage

Seals and drainage must be provided and approved items must be used.

(a) Conduit Seals, Class I, Division 1

1. A seal must be placed in each conduit run which enters the enclosure for a switch, circuit breaker, relay, resistor, fuse, or any item that can cause arcing, sparking, or high temperatures. The seal must be within 18 in. of the enclosure. There is an exception for conduit 1½ in. or smaller under special conditions.

2. If the conduit is 2 in. or larger, the seal

must also be placed within 18 in. of enclosures containing terminals, taps, or splices.

3. If a run of conduit between two enclosures is not more than 36 in., one seal not more than 18 in. from an enclosure is acceptable.

4. A seal is required where a conduit run leaves a Class I, Division 1, location. The conduit must not have a fitting, union, coupling, or box between the seal and point of leaving the Class I, Division 1, location.

(b) Conduit Seals, Class I, Division 2

1. Seals are required for connection to explosion-proof enclosures and must comply with (a)(1) through (a)(3) above.
2. A seal is required when the conduit run leaves this area. The conduit must not have a fitting, union coupling, or box between the seal and point of leaving the Class I, Division 2, location.

(c) Class I, Divisions 1 and 2. These are general rules.

1. The fittings must be approved for Class I locations.
2. The compound must be approved.
3. The thickness of the compound must be at least the trade size of the conduit and not less than ⅝ in.
4. Splices and taps cannot be made in fittings that are used for sealing.
5. Assemblies must be approved for Class I locations.

(d) Cable Seals, Class I, Division 1

(e) Cable Seals, Class I, Division 2

(f) Drainage. In certain cases drainage of accumulated liquid is permitted and even required.

501-6 Switches, Circuit Breakers, Motor Controllers, and Fuses

(a) Class I, Division 1. Must be in an enclosure and the entire assembly must be approved for Class I locations.

(b) Class I, Division 2

1. Must be in enclosures approved for Class I, Division 1, locations unless a general-purpose enclosure is used and it is hermetically sealed or has oil-immersed make-or-break contacts.
2. If not intended to interrupt current, a general-purpose enclosure can be used with a disconnecting or isolating switch for transformers or capacitor banks.
3. Standard plug or cartridge fuses can be used in certain cases, but they must have enclosures approved for the location. If they are oil immersed, they can be placed in general-purpose enclosures.
4. If a distribution panel contains not more than 10 fuses or circuit breakers that are not to be used as switches, the fuses are enclosed, and the circuits are used only for fixed lighting within one room or area, a general-purpose enclosure can be used.
5. Within lighting fixtures, approved cartridge fuses are permitted as supplementary protection.

501-7 Control Transformers and Resistors

Transformers, impedance coils, and resistors are covered by this section.

(a) Class I, Division 1. In this location they must have approved Class I, Division 1, enclosures.

(b) Class I, Division 2. In this location switching mechanisms must be in accordance with Section 501-6(b). General-purpose enclosures can be used for coils and windings. Resistors must have enclosures approved for Class I locations. If the resistor is fixed and the maximum operating temperature is not more than 80% of the ignition temperature of the gas or vapor, a general-purpose enclosure can be used.

501-8 Motors and Generators

(a) Class I, Division 1. In this location they must be either approved for Class I, Division 1, locations or be totally enclosed with a positive pressure ventilation (the arrangement being that the device cannot start until the ventilation has started and 10 volumes of air have been purged from the enclosure) or be totally enclosed filled with inert gas.

(b) Class I, Division 2. In this location you can have open or nonexplosion-proof enclosed motors if they do not have brushes, switching mechanisms, or arc-producing devices. If they do have brushes, switching mechanisms, or arc-producing devices, the motor or generator must be approved for Class I, Division 1, locations or the devices must be in Class I, Division 1, approved enclosures as per Section 501-3(b). A requirement is noted for the surface temperature of space heaters used to prevent condensation.

501-9 Lighting Fixtures

(a) Class I, Division 1. The entire fixture assembly must be approved for a Class I, Division 1, location and be protected against physical damage. Pendant fixtures must be wired and hung through rigid metal conduit or threaded steel intermediate conduit. Stems longer than 12 in. must have additional lateral bracing not more than 12 in. from the end of the stem or a flexible fitting approved for a Class I, Division 1, location. All boxes, fittings, etc., must be approved for Class I, Division 1, locations.

(b) Class I, Division 2. Portable lighting equipment must comply with Class I, Division 1, requirements. There is an exception when it is mounted on a moveable stand and connected by flexible cord. Fixed lighting must be protected against physical damage. If there is danger of falling sparks or hot metal igniting vapors or gases, proper enclosures must be provided. If the operating temperature will exceed 80% of the ignition temperature of the gases or vapors, they must comply with Section 501-9(a)(1) or be "tested and found" not able to ignite the gases or vapors. Pendant fixtures have the same rules as Class I, Division 1, locations. Switches must be in accordance with Section 501-6(b)(1). Starting equipment for electric-discharge lamps must be in accordance with Section 501-7(b) unless it is part of a "thermally protected fluorescent lamp ballast" and the lighting fixture has the approval for this location.

501-10 Utilization Equipment

501-11 Flexible Cords Class I, Divisions 1 and 2

These are permitted only to connect the portable equipment to the fixed part of the system. As such, they must be approved for extra hard usage, contain a grounding conductor, be connected to the supply conductors or terminals in an approved way, ensure that there is no tension applied, and be provided with seals where necessary. Exceptions are made in Sections 501-3(b)(6) and 501-4(b).

501-12 Receptacles and Attachment Plugs, Class I, Divisions 1 and 2

Must be of the grounding type and approved for Class I locations except as provided in Section 501-3(b)(6).

501-13 Conductor Insulation, Class I, Divisions 1 and 2

If the conductors come in contact with vapors or gases, the insulation must be approved for this use or have protection provided by a lead sheath or another approved sheath.

501-14 Signaling, Alarm, Remote-Control, and Communication Systems

501-15 Live Parts, Class I, Divisions 1 and 2

In these locations, live parts are prohibited.

501-16 Grounding, Class I, Divisions 1 and 2

Wiring and equipment must be grounded in accordance with Article 250. Bonding jumpers with proper fitting or other approved means of bonding must be used. Locknut bushings and double locknut types of contacts are not acceptable. If flexible conduit is used it must have internal or external bonding jumpers in parallel with each conduit. It must also comply with the requirements of Section 250-79.

501-17 Surge Protection, Class I, Divisions 1 and 2

ARTICLE 502
CLASS II LOCATIONS

502-1 General

This article refers to areas classified as Class II. There is a definition of dust-ignition-proof. Note that ''explosion-proof'' and ''dust-proof'' are not the same; where dust-proof equipment is required, explosion-proof equipment cannot be required and used unless approved for Class II locations.

502-2 Transformers and Capacitors

(a) Class II, Division 1

1. *Containing liquid that will burn.* They must be installed in approved vaults outside the Divi-

sion 1 location with self-closing fire doors, and have proper ventilation and pressure relief.

2. *Not containing liquid that will burn.* They must be installed in a vault as per Sections 450-41 through 450-48 or have the entire assembly approved for a Class II location.

3. If the area has a metal dust such as magnesium, aluminum, etc., you cannot install a transformer or capacitor.

(b) Class II, Division 2

1. *Containing liquid that will burn.* Must be installed in vaults as per Sections 450-41 through 450-48.

2. *Containing Askarel.* If it is larger than 25 kVA, it must have a pressure relief vent, have a way of absorbing gases from inside, and have an air space of at least 6 in. between the case and any combustible material.

3. *Dry-type transformers.* Must be in vaults or not operate over 600 V, with the windings and terminals enclosed without ventilating or other openings.

502-4 Wiring Methods

(a) Class II, Division 1. Only threaded rigid metal conduit, threaded steel intermediate metal conduit, or Type MI cable can be used. Boxes and fittings can have no openings and have threaded bosses so that no dust can come in. If used where the dust is combustible electrically conductive, they must be approved for Class II locations. If a flexible connection must be used, it has to be either a dust-tight flexible connector, liquidtight flexible metal conduit, or a flexible cord for extra-hard usage and bushed fittings. The flexible cord must have a grounding conductor.

(b) Class II, Division 2. Methods permitted are rigid metal conduit, intermediate metal conduit, electrical metal tubing, dust-tight wireways, or

Type MI, MC, or SNM cable that have approved termination fittings or Type PLTC, MC, or SNM under certain conditions. There is one exception. Also, wireways, fittings, and boxes must minimize the entrance of dust by the use of close-fitting covers and no openings. The requirements for flexible connections are the same as for Class II, Division 1.

502-5 Sealing, Class II, Divisions 1 and 2

If a raceway connects two enclosures, one being dust-ignition-proof, the other not, provision must be made to prevent dust from getting into the dust-ignition-proof enclosures. This can be done with seals, a minimum of 10 ft of horizontal raceway, or a minimum of 5 ft of vertical raceway. If the dust-ignition-proof enclosure is connected to one in an unclassified area, a seal is not required.

502-6 Switches, Circuit Breakers, Motor Controllers, and Fuses

(a) Class II, Division 1. Their enclosures must be dust-ignition-proof. If the dust is a hazardous metal (magnesium, etc.), the enclosure must be approved for this specific type of location. If they are not installed where there is electrically conductive dust, are not to interrupt current, and have no fuses, the enclosure only has to be tight so as to keep the entrance of dust to a minimum and have no openings, as well as close-fitting or telescoping covers.

(b) Class II, Division 2. The enclosures only have to be dust-tight.

502-7 Control Transformers and Resistors

(a) Class II, Division 1. The enclosures must be dust-ignition-proof approved for a Class II location. If they are installed in a location with hazardous metal dust (magnesium, etc.), the enclosure must be approved for this specific type of location.

(b) Class II, Division 2. In these locations, the switching mechanisms must have a dust-tight enclosure. If they are in the same location as the switching mechanism, they must have tight metal enclosures with no openings. Resistors must have approved Class II enclosures unless their temperature is not higher than 248°F and they are either nonadjustable or part of an automatic timing system. In that case the enclosures have only to be tight with no openings.

502-8 Motors and Generators

(a) Class II, Division 1. They must be either totally enclosed pipe-ventilated and meet the temperature restrictions of Section 502-1 or be approved for locations classified as Class II, Division 1.

(b) Class II, Division 2. They must be either totally enclosed pipe-ventilated, totally enclosed fan cooled, totally enclosed nonventilated or dust-ignition-proof with full load external temperature in accordance with Section 500-3(d). There are exceptions for these types of motors if the authority having jurisdiction feels that the machines are easily cleaned and maintained and there will not be a large accumulation of dust.

502-9 Ventilating Piping

The piping must (1) not be lighter than No. 24MSG, (2) be screened at the outside ends, (3) lead to the outside of the building and have clean air available, and (4) be protected against corrosion and physical damage. In addition, it must comply with:

(a) Class II, Division 1. The pipes must be entirely dust-tight. They must also be either riveted and soldered, bolted and soldered, welded, or be dust-tight by another effective means.

(b) Class II, Division 2. The pipes must be tight enough to prevent the entrance of dust in appreciable quantities.

502-10 Utilization Equipment

(a) Class II, Division 1. Must be approved for Class II locations. If hazardous dust is present, it must also be approved for that location.

(b) Class II, Division 2. Heaters must be approved for Class II locations. There is one exception. Motors must be in accordance with Section 502-8(b). Dust-tight enclosures are required for circuit breakers, switches, and fuses. Section 502-7 is applied to transformers, impedance coils, and resistors.

502-11 Lighting Fixtures

(a) Class II, Division 1. The fixtures must be approved for Class II locations and additionally for hazardous metal dust if so located. They must be protected against physical damage. Pendant fixtures must be suspended using threaded rigid metal conduit, threaded steel intermediate metal conduit, or approved chains or other means. If the stem is longer than 12 in., it must be braced within 12 in. from the lower end or have a flexible fitting not more than 12 in. from the upper end. If conduit is not used for the wiring, the cord must be approved for hard usage and proper seals must be used. All boxes, fittings, etc., must be approved for Class II locations.

(b) Class II, Division 2. Portable lighting equipment must be approved for Class II locations. A fixed lighting fixture must only minimize the collection of dust and prevent the escape of sparks. It must also have maximum wattage permitted for temperatures in accordance with Section 500-3(d). Fixtures in these locations must also be protected against physical damage. Requirements for pendant fixtures in Division 2 are basically the same as for Division 1. One difference is that seals are not required. The requirements of Section 502-7(b) apply here for starters and control equipment for electric-discharge lamps.

502-12 Flexible Cords, Class II, Divisions 1 and 2

502-13 Receptacles and Attachment Plugs

(a) Class II, Division 1. Must be approved for Class II locations and have a grounding conductor connection.

(b) Class II, Division 2. Must also have a grounding conductor connection. They cannot permit the supply circuit to open with exposed live parts.

502-14 Signaling, Alarm, Remote-Control, and Communication Systems, Meters, Instruments and Relays

502-15 Live Parts, Class II, Divisions 1 and 2

Live parts are not permitted to be exposed.

502-16 Grounding, Class II, Divisions 1 and 2

Ground, in accordance with Article 250, all wiring and equipment.

(a) Bonding jumpers with proper fittings or other approved means must be used. Locknut-bushings and double locknut contacts alone are not permitted.

(b) If flexible conduit is used, it must have internal or external bonding jumpers in parallel with each conduit. It must also comply with the requirements of Section 250-79.

502-17 Surge Protection, Class II, Divisions 1 and 2

ARTICLE 503
CLASS III LOCATIONS

503-1 General

Maximum surface temperatures for equipment permitted under operating conditions are 329°F for normal operation or 248°F if the equipment can be overloaded.

503-2 Transformers and Capacitors, Class II, Divisions 1 and 2

Must be in accordance with Section 502-2(b).

503-3 Wiring Methods

(a) Class III, Division 1. Use only rigid metal conduit, rigid nonmetallic conduit, intermediate metal conduit, electrical metallic tubing, dust-tight wireways or Type MI, MC or SNM cables with approved fittings. Fittings and boxes must be dust tight. Refer to this section for the requirements for flexible connections.

(b) Class III, Division 2. Same requirements as Division 1. An exception is made for storage areas with no machinery, where open wire on insulators can be used complying with Article 320, specifically Section 320-14.

503-4 Switches, Circuit Breakers, Motor Controllers and Fuses Class III, Divisions 1 and 2

These devices must have dust-tight metal enclosures.

503-5 Control Transformers and Resistors, Class III, Divisions 1 and 2

Must be in dust-tight enclosures complying with temperature limitations in Section 503-1.

503-6 Motors and Generators, Class III, Divisions 1 and 2

(a) Class III, Division 1. Must be totally enclosed pipe ventilated, totally enclosed nonventilated, or totally enclosed fan cooled. There is an exception where the authority having jurisdiction will permit it.

503-7 Ventilating Piping, Class III, Division 1 and 2

Must be metal at least No. 24MSG or equal noncombustible material, have physical damage protection, go directly outside to clean air, and be screened. The pipes must be tight enough to prevent ''appreciable quantities'' of fibers or flyings from getting in and sparks getting out.

503-8 Utilization Equipment, Class III, Divisions 1 and 2

Heaters: approved for Class III locations. Motors: Section 503-6. Switches, circuit breakers, motor controllers, and fuses: Section 503-4.

503-9 Lighting Fixtures, Class III, Divisions 1 and 2

Protect against physical damage. Prevent entrance of fibers or flyings or escape of sparks. Pendant stems must be threaded rigid metal conduit, threaded intermediate metal conduit, or threaded metal tubing. Chains with approved fittings can be used for suspending fixtures. The same rules apply for bracing stems over 12 in. long as Class II. Portable lamps must have handles, guards, and the lampholders have no switches, exposed parts, or receptacles.

503-10 Flexible Cords, Class III, Divisions 1 and 2

They must be approved for extra hard usage, have a grounding conductor, be connected in an approved manner, be supported so as to prevent tension on the connections, and have provisions to prevent fibers or flyings from entering the boxes or fittings.

503-11 Receptacles and Attachment Plugs, Class III, Divisions 1 and 2

They must be of the grounding type, and designed to prevent the escape of sparks or molten particles and minimize the entry of fibers or flyings. An exception is provided where permitted by the authority having jurisdiction.

503-12 Signaling, Alarm, Remote-Control, and Local Loud Speaker Inter-communication Systems, Class III, Divisions 1 and 2

503-13 Electric Cranes, Hoists, and Similar Equipment, Class III, Divisions 1 and 2

503-14 Storage-Battery Charging Equipment, Class III, Divisions 1 and 2

503-15 Live Parts, Class III, Divisions 1 and 2

No exposed live parts permitted.

503-16 Grounding, Class III, Divisions 1 and 2

As per Article 250. Also, the same requirements hold true for bonding and grounding as in Sections 501-16, and 502-16.

ARTICLE 510 HAZARDOUS (CLASSIFIED) LOCATIONS, SPECIFIC

Articles 511 through 517 cover specific locations that might be hazardous. The following article titles are listed for reference: **Article 511**—Commercial Garages, Repair and Storage; **Article 513**—Aircraft Hangars; **Article 514**—Gasoline Dispensing and Service Stations; **Article 515**—Bulk Storage Plants; **Article 516**—Spray Application, Dipping and Coating Processes; **Article 517**—Health Care Facilities; **Article 518**—Places of Assembly; **Article 520**—Theaters and Similar Locations; **Article 530**—Motion Picture and Television Studios and Similar Locations; **Article 540**—Motion Picture Projectors; **Article 545**—Manufactured Building; **Article 547**—Agricultural Buildings; **Article 550**—Mobile Homes and Mobile Home Parks; **Article 551**—Recreational Vehicles and Recreational Vehicle Parks; **Article 553**—Floating Buildings; **Article 555**—Marinas and Boatyards.

6, 7, and 8

CHAPTER 6 SPECIAL EQUIPMENT

Article 600—Electric Signs and Outline Lighting; **Article 604**—Manufactured Wiring Systems; **Article 605**—Office Furnishings; **Article 610**—Cranes and Hoists; **Article 620**—Elevators, Dumbwaiters, Escalators, and Moving Walks; **Article 630**—Electric Welders; **Article 640**—Sound-Recording and Similar Equipment; **Article 645**—Electronic Computer/Data Processing Systems; **Article 650**—Organs; **Article 660**—X-Ray Equipment; **Article 665**—Induction and Dielectric Heating Equipment; **Article 668**—Electrolytic Cells; **Article 669**—Electroplating; **Article 670**—Industrial Machinery; **Article 675**—Electrically Driven or Controlled Irrigation Machines; **Article 680**—Swimming Pools, Fountains, and Similar Installations; **Article 685**—

Note: Chapters 6, 7, and 8 are listed here with article titles for reference purposes.

Integrated Electrical Systems, **Article 690**—Solar Photovoltaic Systems.

CHAPTER 7
SPECIAL CONDITIONS

Article 700—Emergency Systems; **Article 701**—Legally Required Standby Systems; **Article 702**—Optional Standby Systems; **Article 705**—Interconnected Electric Power Production Sources; **Article 710**—Over 600 Volts, Nominal—General; **Article 720**—Circuits and Equipment Operating at Less than 50 Volts; **Article 725**—Class 1, Class 2, and Class 3 Remote-Control, Signaling, and Power-Limited Circuits; **Article 760**—Fire Protective Signaling Systems; **Article 770**—Optical Fiber Cables; **Article 780**—Closed-Loop and Programmed Power Distribution.

CHAPTER 8
COMMUNICATIONS SYSTEMS

Article 800—Communication Circuits; **Article 810**—Radio and Television Equipment; **Article 820**—Community Antenna Television and Radio Distribution Systems.

9

TABLES AND EXAMPLES

A. TABLES

Notes to Tables

1. Tables 3A, 3B and 3C apply only to complete conduit or tubing systems and are not intended to apply to sections of conduit or tubing used to protect exposed wiring from physical damage.
2. Equipment grounding or bonding conductors, when installed, shall be included when calculating conduit or tubing fill. The actual dimensions of the equipment grounding or bonding conductor (insulated or bare) shall be used in the calculation.
3. When conduit or tubing nipples having a maximum length not to exceed 24 inches (610 mm) are installed between boxes, cabinets, and similar enclosures, the nipple shall be permitted to be filled to 60 percent of its total cross-sectional area, and Note 8 of Tables 310-16 through 310-19 does not apply to this condition.
4. For conductors not included in Chapter 9,

such as compact or multiconductor cables, the actual dimensions shall be used.

5. See Table 1 for allowable percentage of conduit or tubing fill.

Table 1 is based on common conditions of proper cabling and alignment of conductors where the length of the pull and the number of bends are within reasonable limits. It should be recognized that for certain conditions a larger size conduit or a lesser conduit fill should be considered.

TABLE 1 Percent of Cross Section of Conduit and Tubing for Conductors

Number of Conductors	*1*	*2*	*3*	*4*	*Over 4*
All conductor types except lead-covered	53	31	40	40	40
Lead-covered conductors	55	30	40	38	35

See Table 2 for fixture wires.

Note 1: See Tables 3A, 3B, and 3C for number of conductors all of the same size in trade sizes of conduit ½ inch through 6 inch.

Note 2: For conductors larger than 750 MCM or for combinations of conductors of different sizes, use Tables 4 through 8, Chapter 9, for dimensions of conductors, conduit, and tubing.

Note 3: Where the calculated number of conductors, all of the same size, includes a decimal fraction, the next higher whole number shall be used where this decimal is 0.8 or larger.

Note 4: When bare conductors are permitted by other sections of this Code, the dimensions for bare conductors in Table 8 of Chapter 9 shall be permitted.

Note 5: A multiconductor cable of two or more conductors shall be treated as a single conductor cable for calculating percentage conduit fill area. For cables that have elliptical cross section, the cross-sectional area calculation shall be based on using the major diameter of the ellipse as a circle diameter.

TABLE 2 Maximum Number of Fixture Wires in Trade Sizes of Conduit or Tubing

(40 Percent Fill Based on Individual Diameters)

Conduit Trade Size (Inches)	*½*					*¾*					*1*					*1¼*					*1½*					*2*				
Wire Types	*18*	*16*	*14*	*12*	*10*	*18*	*16*	*14*	*12*	*10*	*18*	*16*	*14*	*12*	*10*	*18*	*16*	*14*	*12*	*10*	*18*	*16*	*14*	*12*	*10*	*18*	*16*	*14*	*12*	*10*
PTF, PTFF, PGFF, PGF, PFF, PF, PAF, PAFF, ZF, ZFF	23	18	14			40	31	24			65	50	39			115	90	70			157	122	95			257	200	156		
TFFN, TFN	19	15				34	26				55	43				97	76				132	104				216	169			
SF-1	16					29					47					83					114					186				
SFF-1	15					26					43					76					104					169				
TF	11	10				20	18				32	30				57	53				79	72				129	118			

RFH-1	11					20					32					57					79					129				
TFF	11	10				20	17				32	27				56	49				77	66				126	109			
AF	11	9	7	4	3	19	16	12	7	5	31	26	20	11	8	55	46	36	19	15	75	63	49	27	20	123	104	81	44	34
SFF-2	9	7	6			16	12	10			27	20	17			47	36	30			65	49	42			106	81	68		
SF-2	9	8	6			16	14	11			27	23	18			47	40	32			65	55	43			106	90	71		
FFH-2	9	7				15	12				25	19				44	34				60	46				99	75			
RFH-2	7	5				12	10				20	16				36	28				49	38				80	62			
KF-1, KFF-1, KF-2, KFF-2	36	32	22	14	9	64	55	39	25	17	103	89	63	41	28	182	158	111	73	49	248	216	152	100	67	406	353	248	163	110

TABLE 3A Maximum Number of Conductors in Trade Sizes of Conduit or Tubing

Type Letters	Conductor Size AWG, MCM	½	¾	1	1¼	1½	2	2½	3	3½	4	5	6
Conduit Trade Size (Inches)		½	¾	1	1¼	1½	2	2½	3	3½	4	5	6
TW, RUH,	14	9	15	25	44	60	99	142					
	12	7	12	19	35	47	78	111	171				
XHHW (14 through 8)	10	5	9	15	26	36	60	85	131	176			
	8	2	4	7	12	17	28	40	62	84	108		
RHW and RHH	14	6	10	16	29	40	65	93	143	192			
(without outer	12	4	8	13	24	32	53	76	117	157			
covering),	10	4	6	11	19	26	43	61	95	127	163		
THW	8	1	3	5	10	13	22	32	49	66	85	133	
TW,	6	1	2	4	7	10	16	23	36	48	62	97	141
	4	1	1	3	5	7	12	17	27	36	47	73	106
THW,	3	1	1	2	4	6	10	15	23	31	40	63	91

	2	1	1	2	4	5	9	13	20	27	34	54	78
	1		1	1	3	4	6	9	14	19	25	39	57
FEPB (6 through 2), RHW and RHH (without outer covering)	1/0		1	1	2	3	5	8	12	16	21	33	49
	2/0		1	1	1	3	5	7	10	14	18	29	41
	3/0		1	1	1	2	4	6	9	12	15	24	35
	4/0			1	1	1	3	5	7	10	13	20	29
	250			1	1	1	2	4	6	8	10	16	23
	300			1	1	1	2	3	5	7	9	14	20
	350				1	1	1	3	4	6	8	12	18
	400				1	1	1	2	4	5	7	11	16
	500				1	1	1	1	3	4	6	9	14
	600					1	1	1	3	4	5	7	11
	700					1	1	1	2	3	4	7	10
	750					1	1	1	2	3	4	6	9

Based on Table 1, Chapter 9.

Note: This table is for concentric stranded conductors only. For cables with compact conductors, the dimensions in Table 5A shall be used.

TABLE 3B Maximum Number of Conductors in Trade Sizes of Conduit or Tubing

Conduit Trade Size (Inches)		*1/2*	*3/4*	*1*	*1 1/4*	*1 1/2*	*2*	*2 1/2*	*3*	*3 1/2*	*4*	*5*	*6*
Type Letters	*Conductor Size AWG, MCM*												
THWN,	14	13	24	39	69	94	154						
	12	10	18	29	51	70	114	164					
	10	6	11	18	32	44	73	104	160				
	8	3	5	9	16	22	36	51	79	106	136		
THHN,	6	1	4	6	11	15	26	37	57	76	98	154	
FEP (14 through 2),	4	1	2	4	7	9	16	22	35	47	60	94	137
FEPB (14 through 8),	3	1	1	3	6	8	13	19	29	39	51	80	116
PFA (14 through 4/0)	2	1	1	3	5	7	11	16	25	33	43	67	97
PFAH (14 through 4/0)	1		1	1	3	5	8	12	18	25	32	50	72

Z (14 through 4/0) XHHW (4 through 500MCM)	1/0		1	1	3	4	7	10	15	21	27	42	61
	2/0		1	1	2	3	6	8	13	17	22	35	51
	3/0		1	1	1	3	5	7	11	14	18	29	42
	4/0		1	1	1	2	4	6	9	12	15	24	35
	250			1	1	1	3	4	7	10	12	20	28
	300			1	1	1	3	4	6	8	11	17	24
	350			1	1	1	2	3	5	7	9	15	21
	400				1	1	1	3	5	6	8	13	19
	500				1	1	1	2	4	5	7	11	16
	600				1	1	1	1	3	4	5	9	13
	700					1	1	1	3	4	5	8	11
	750					1	1	1	2	3	4	7	11
XHHW	6	1	3	5	9	13	21	30	47	63	81	128	185
	600				1	1	1	1	3	4	5	9	13
	700					1	1	1	3	4	5	7	11
	750					1	1	1	2	3	4	7	10

Based on Table 1, Chapter 9.

Note: This table is for concentric stranded conductors only. For cables with compact conductors, the dimensions in Table 5A shall be used.

TABLE 3C Maximum Number of Conductors in Trade Sizes of Conduit or Tubing

Conduit Trade Size (Inches)		*½*	*¾*	*1*	*1¼*	*1½*	*2*	*2½*	*3*	*3½*	*4*	*5*	*6*
Type Letters	*Conductor Size AWG, MCM*												
RHW	14	3	6	10	18	25	41	58	90	121	155		
	12	3	5	9	15	21	35	50	77	103	132		
	10	2	4	7	13	18	29	41	64	86	110		
	8	1	2	4	7	9	16	22	35	47	60	94	137
RHH	6	1	1	2	5	6	11	15	24	32	41	64	93
	4	1	1	1	3	5	8	12	18	24	31	50	72
(with	3	1	1	1	3	4	7	10	16	22	28	44	63
outer	2		1	1	3	4	6	9	14	19	24	38	56
covering)	1		1	1	1	3	5	7	11	14	18	29	42

1/0		1	1	1	2	4	6	9	12	16	25	37
2/0			1	1	1	3	5	8	11	14	22	32
3/0			1	1	1	3	4	7	9	12	19	28
4/0			1	1	1	2	4	6	8	10	16	24
250				1	1	1	3	5	6	8	13	19
300				1	1	1	3	4	5	7	11	17
350				1	1	1	2	4	5	6	10	15
400				1	1	1	1	3	4	6	9	14
500				1	1	1	1	3	4	5	8	11
600					1	1	1	2	3	4	6	9
700					1	1	1	1	3	3	6	8
750						1	1	1	3	3	5	8

Based on Table 1, Chapter 9.
Note: This table is for concentric stranded conductors only. For cables with compact conductors, the dimensions in Table 5A shall be used.

Tables 4 through 8. Tables 4 through 8 give the nominal size of conductors and conduit or tubing for use in computing size of conduit or tubing for various combinations of conductors. The dimensions represent average conditions only, and variations will be found in dimensions of conductors and conduits of different manufacture.

TABLE 4 Dimensions and Percent Area of Conduit and of Tubing

Areas of Conduit or Tubing for the Combinations of Wires Permitted in Table 1, Chapter 9.

Trade Size	Internal Diameter Inches	*Area—Square Inches*								
			Not Lead Covered			*Lead Covered*				
		Total 100%	*2 Cond. 31%*	*Over 2 Cond. 40%*	*1 Cond. 53%*	*1 Cond. 55%*	*2 Cond. 30%*	*3 Cond. 40%*	*4 Cond. 38%*	*Over 4 Cond. 35%*
½	.622	.30	.09	.12	.16	.17	.09	.12	.11	.11
¾	.824	.53	.16	.21	.28	.29	.16	.21	.20	.19
1	1.049	.86	.27	.34	.46	.47	.26	.34	.33	.30

1¼	1.380	1.50	.47	.60	.80	.83	.45	.60	.57	.53
1½	1.610	2.04	.63	.82	1.08	1.12	.61	.82	.78	.71
2	2.067	3.36	1.04	1.34	1.78	1.85	1.01	1.34	1.28	1.18
2½	2.469	4.79	1.48	1.92	2.54	2.63	1.44	1.92	1.82	1.68
3	3.068	7.38	2.29	2.95	3.91	4.06	2.21	2.95	2.80	2.58
3½	3.548	9.90	3.07	3.96	5.25	5.44	2.97	3.96	3.76	3.47
4	4.026	12.72	3.94	5.09	6.74	7.00	3.82	5.09	4.83	4.45
5	5.047	20.00	6.20	8.00	10.60	11.00	6.00	8.00	7.60	7.00
6	6.065	28.89	8.96	11.56	15.31	15.89	8.67	11.56	10.98	10.11

TABLE 5 Dimensions of Rubber-Covered and Thermoplastic-Covered Conductors

Size AWG MCM	Types RFH-2, RH, RHH,*** RHW,*** SF-2		Types TF, THW,† TW		Types TFN, THHN, THWN		Types**** FEP, FEPB, FEPW, TFE, PF, PFA, PFAH, PGF, PTF, Z, ZF, ZFF		Type XHHW, ZW††		Types KF-1, KF-2, KFF-1, KFF-2	
	Approx. Diam. Inches	Approx. Area Sq. In.	Approx. Diam. Inches	Approx. Area Sq. In.	Approx. Diam. Inches	Approx. Area Sq. In.	Approx. Diam. Inches	Approx. Area Sq. Inches	Approx. Diam. Inches	Approx. Area Sq. In.	Approx. Diam. Sq. In.	Approx. Area Sq. In.
Col. 1	Col. 2	Col. 3	Col. 4	Col. 5	Col. 6	Col. 7	Col. 8	Col. 9	Col. 10	Col. 11	Col. 12	Col. 13
18	.146	.0167	.106	.0088	.089	.0062	.081	.0052	—	—	.065	.0033
16	.158	.0196	.118	.0109	.100	.0079	.092	.0066	—	—	.070	.0038

14	30 mils	.171	.0230	.131	.0135	.105	.0087	.105	.105	.0087	.0087	—	—	.083	.0054
14	45 mils	.204*	.0327*	—	—	—	—	—	—	—	—	—	—	—	—
14	—	—	—	.162†	.0206†	—	—	—	—	—	—	.129	.0131	—	—
12	30 mils	.188	.0278	.148	.0172	.122	.0117	.121	.121	.0115	.0115	—	—	.102	.0082
12	45 mils	.221*	.0384*	—	—	—	—	—	—	—	—	—	—	—	—
12	—	—	—	.179†	.0252†	—	—	—	—	—	—	.146	.0167	—	—
10	—	.242	.0460	.168	.0222	.153	.0184	.142	.142	.0158	.0158	—	—	.124	.0121
10	—	—	—	.199†	.0311†	—	—	—	—	—	—	.166	.0216	—	—
8	—	.328	.0845	.245	.0471	.218	.0373	.206	.186	.0333	.0272	—	—	—	—
8	—	—	—	.276†	.0598†	—	—	—	—	—	—	.241	.0456	—	—
6		.397	.1238	.323	.0819	.257	.0519	.244	.302	.0468	.0716	.282	.0625	—	—
4		.452	.1605	.372	.1087	.328	.0845	.292	.350	.0670	.0962	.328	.0845	—	—
3		.481	.1817	.401	.1263	.356	.0995	.320	.378	.0804	.1122	.356	.0995	—	—
2		.513	.2067	.433	.1473	.388	.1182	.352	.410	.0973	.1320	.388	.1182	—	—
1		.588	.2715	.508	.2027	.450	.1590	.420	—	.1385	—	.450	.1590	—	—
1/0		.629	.3107	.549	.2367	.491	.1893	.462	—	.1676	—	.491	.1893	—	—
2/0		.675	.3578	.595	.2781	.537	.2265	.498	—	.1948	—	.537	.2265	—	—
3/0		.727	.4151	.647	.3288	.588	.2715	.560	—	.2463	—	.588	.2715	—	—
4/0		.785	.4840	.705	.3904	.646	.3278	.618	—	.3000	—	.646	.3278	—	—

TABLE 5 (Continued)

	*Types RFH-2, RH, RHH,*** RHW,*** SF-2*		*Types TF, THW,† TW*		*Types TFN, THHN, THWN*		*Types**** FEP, FEPB, FEPW, TFE, PF, PFA, PFAH, PGF, PTF, Z, ZF, ZFF*		*Type XHHW, ZW††*	
Size AWG MCM	*Approx. Diam. Inches*	*Approx. Area Sq. In.*	*Approx. Diam. Inches*	*Approx. Area Sq. In.*	*Approx. Diam. Inches*	*Approx. Area Sq. In.*	*Approx. Diam. Inches*	*Approx. Area Sq. Inches*	*Approx. Diam. Inches*	*Approx. Area Sq. In.*
Col. 1	*Col. 2*	*Col. 3*	*Col. 4*	*Col. 5*	*Col. 6*	*Col. 7*	*Col. 8*	*Col. 9*	*Col. 10*	*Col. 11*
250	.868	.5917	.788	.4877	.716	.4026	—	—	.716	.4026
300	.933	.6837	.843	.5581	.771	.4669	—	—	.771	.4669
350	.985	.7620	.895	.6291	.822	.5307	—	—	.822	.5307
400	1.032	.8365	.942	.6969	.869	.5931	—	—	.869	.5931
500	1.119	.9834	1.029	.8316	.955	.7163	—	—	.955	.7163

600	1.233	1.1940	1.143	1.0261	1.058	.8791	—	—	1.073	.9043
700	1.304	1.3355	1.214	1.1575	1.129	1.0011	—	—	1.145	1.0297
750	1.339	1.4082	1.249	1.2252	1.163	1.0623	—	—	1.180	1.0936
800	1.372	1.4784	1.282	1.2908	1.196	1.1234	—	—	1.210	1.1499
900	1.435	1.6173	1.345	1.4208	1.259	1.2449	—	—	1.270	1.2668
1000	1.494	1.7530	1.404	1.5482	1.317	1.3623	—	—	1.330	1.3893
1250	1.676	2.2062	1.577	1.9532	—	—	—	—	1.500	1.7671
1500	1.801	2.5475	1.702	2.2751	—	—	—	—	1.620	2.0612
1750	1.916	2.8832	1.817	2.5930	—	—	—	—	1.740	2.3779
2000	2.021	3.2079	1.922	2.9013	—	—	—	—	1.840	2.6590

* The dimensions of Types RHH and RHW.

† Dimensions of THW in sizes No. 14 to No. 8. No. 6 THW and larger is the same dimension as TW.

*** Dimensions of RHH and RHW without outer covering are the same as THW No. 18 to No. 10, solid; No. 8 and larger, stranded.

**** In Columns 8 and 9 the values shown for sizes No. 1 thru 4/0 are for TFE and Z only. The right-hand values in Columns 8 and 9 are for FEPB, Z, ZF, and ZFF only.

†† No. 14 through No. 2.

TABLE 5A Aluminum Building Wire Nominal Dimensions* and Areas

Bare Conductor**			Type THW		Type THHN		Type XHHW		
Size AWG or MCM	Number of Standards	Diam. Inches	Approx. Diam. Inches	Approx. Area Sq. In.	Approx. Diam. Inches	Approx. Area Sq. In.	Approx. Diam. Inches	Approx. Area Sq. In.	Size AWG or MCM
8	7	.134	.255	.0510	—	—	.224	.0394	8
6	7	.169	.290	.0660	.240	.0452	.260	.0530	6
4	7	.213	.335	.0881	.305	.0730	.305	.0730	4
2	7	.268	.390	.1194	.360	.1017	.360	.1017	2
1	19	.299	.465	.1698	.415	.1352	.415	.1352	1
1/0	19	.336	.500	.1963	.450	.1590	.450	.1590	1/0
2/0	19	.376	.545	.2332	.495	.1924	.490	.1885	2/0
3/0	19	.423	.590	.2733	.540	.2290	.540	.2290	3/0
4/0	19	.475	.645	.3267	.595	.2780	.590	.2733	4/0

250	37	.520	.725	.4128	.670	.3525	.660	.3421	250
300	37	.570	.775	.4717	.720	.4071	.715	.4015	300
350	37	.616	.820	.5281	.770	.4656	.760	.4536	350
400	37	.659	.865	.5876	.815	.5216	.800	.5026	400
500	37	.736	.940	.6939	.885	.6151	.880	.6082	500
600	61	.813	1.050	.8659	.985	.7620	.980	.7542	600
700	61	.877	1.110	.9676	1.050	.8659	1.050	.8659	700
750	61	.908	1.150	1.0386	1.075	.9076	1.090	.9331	750
1000	61	1.060	1.285	1.2968	1.255	1.2370	1.230	1.1882	1000

* Dimensions are from industry sources

** Compact conductor per ASTM B 400

TABLE 6 Dimensions of Lead-Covered Conductors:

Types RL and RHL

Size AWG-MCM	Single Conductor		Two Conductor		Three Conductor	
	Diam. Inches	*Area Sq. In.*	*Diam. Inches*	*Area Sq. In.*	*Diam. Inches*	*Area Sq. In.*
14	.28	.062	.28 × .47	.115	.59	.273
12	.29	.066	.31 × .54	.146	.62	.301
10	.35	.096	35 × .59	.180	.68	.363
8 sol.	.41	.132	.41 × .71	.255	.82	.528
8 str.	.43	.145	.43 × .75	.282	.86	.581
6	.49	.188	.49 × .86	.369	.97	.738
4	.55	.237	.54 × .96	.457	1.08	.916
2	.60	.283	.61 × 1.08	.578	1.21	1.146
1	.67	.352	.70 × 1.23	.756	1.38	1.49

1/0	.71	.396	.74 × 1.32	.859	1.47	1.70
2/0	.76	.454	.79 × 1.41	.980	1.57	1.94
3/0	.81	.515	.84 × 1.52	1.123	1.69	2.24
4/0	.87	.593	.90 × 1.64	1.302	1.85	2.68
250	.98	.754	—	—	2.02	3.20
300	1.04	.85	—	—	2.15	3.62
350	1.10	.95	—	—	2.26	4.02
400	1.14	1.02	—	—	2.40	4.52
500	1.23	1.18	—	—	2.59	5.28

The above cables are limited to straight runs or with nominal offsets equivalent to not more than two quarter bends.
Note: No. 14 through No. 10, solid conductors; No. 8, solid or stranded conductors; No. 6 and larger, stranded conductors.

TABLE 7 Dimensions of Asbestos-Varnished-Cambric Insulated Conductors

Types AVA, AVB, and AVL

Size AWG, MCM	Type AVA		Type AVB		Type AVL	
	Approx. Diam. Inches	Approx. Area Sq. In.	Approx. Diam. Inches	Approx. Area Sq. In.	Approx. Diam. Inches	Approx. Area Sq. In.
14	.245	.047	.205	.033	.320	.080
12	.265	.055	.225	.040	.340	.091
10	.285	.064	.245	.047	.360	.102
8 sol.	.310	.075	.270	.057	.390	.119
8 str.	.325	.083	.285	.064	.390	.119
6	.395	.122	.345	.094	.430	.145
4	.445	.155	.395	.123	.480	.181
2	.505	.200	.460	.166	.570	.255
1	.585	.268	.540	.229	.620	.300
1/0	.625	.307	.580	.264	.660	.341
2/0	.670	.353	.625	.307	.705	.390
3/0	.720	.406	.675	.358	.755	.447
4/0	.780	.478	.735	.425	.815	.521

250	.885	.616	.855	.572	.955	.715
300	.940	.692	.910	.649	1.010	.800
350	.995	.778	.965	.731	1.060	.885
400	1.040	.850	1.010	.800	1.105	.960
500	1.125	.995	1.095	.945	1.190	1.118
550	1.165	1.065	1.135	1.01	1.265	1.26
600	1.205	1.140	1.175	1.09	1.305	1.34
650	1.240	1.21	1.210	1.15	1.340	1.41
700	1.275	1.28	1.245	1.22	1.375	1.49
750	1.310	1.35	1.280	1.29	1.410	1.57
800	1.345	1.42	1.315	1.36	1.440	1.63
850	1.375	1.49	1.345	1.43	1.470	1.70
900	1.405	1.55	1.375	1.49	1.505	1.78
950	1.435	1.62	1.405	1.55	1.535	1.85
1000	1.465	1.69	1.435	1.62	1.565	1.93

Note: No. 14 to No. 10, solid; No. 8, solid or stranded; No. 6 and larger, stranded; except AVL where all sizes are stranded.

Varnished-Cambric Insulated Conductors, Type V. The insulation thickness for varnished-cambric conductors, Type V, is the same as for rubber-covered conductors, Type RHH, except for No. 8, which has 45-mil insulation for varnished-cambric, and 60-mil insulation for rubber-covered conductors. See Table 310-13. Therefore, Table 3C shall be permitted to be used for the number of varnished-cambric insulated conductors in a conduit or tubing.

TABLE 8 Conductor Properties

		Conductors				DC Resistance at 75°C (167°F)		
		Stranding		Overall		Copper		Aluminum
Size AWG/MCM	Area Cir. Mils	Quantity	Diam. In.	Diam. In.	Area $In.^2$	Uncoated ohm/MFT	Coated ohm/MFT	ohm/MFT
18	1620	1	—	0.040	0.001	7.77	8.08	12.8
18	1620	7	0.015	0.046	0.002	7.95	8.45	13.1
16	2580	1	—	0.051	0.002	4.89	5.08	8.05
16	2580	7	0.019	0.058	0.003	4.99	5.29	8.21
14	4110	1	—	0.064	0.003	3.07	3.19	5.06
14	4110	7	0.024	0.073	0.004	3.14	3.26	5.17
12	6530	1	—	0.081	0.005	1.93	2.01	3.18
12	6530	7	0.030	0.092	0.006	1.98	2.05	3.25

10	10380	1	—	0.102	0.008	1.21	1.26	2.00
10	10380	7	0.038	0.116	0.011	1.24	1.29	2.04
8	16510	1	—	0.128	0.013	0.764	0.786	1.26
8	16510	7	0.049	0.146	0.017	0.778	0.809	1.28
6	26240	7	0.061	0.184	0.027	0.491	0.510	0.808
4	41740	7	0.077	0.232	0.042	0.308	0.321	0.508
3	52620	7	0.087	0.260	0.053	0.245	0.254	0.403
2	66360	7	0.097	0.292	0.067	0.194	0.201	0.319
1	83690	19	0.066	0.332	0.087	0.154	0.160	0.253
1/0	105600	19	0.074	0.373	0.109	0.122	0.127	0.201
2/0	133100	19	0.084	0.419	0.138	0.0967	0.101	0.159
3/0	167800	19	0.094	0.470	0.173	0.0766	0.0797	0.126
4/0	211600	19	0.106	0.528	0.219	0.0608	0.0626	0.100
250	—	37	0.082	0.575	0.260	0.0515	0.0535	0.0847
300	—	37	0.090	0.630	0.312	0.0429	0.0446	0.0707
350	—	37	0.097	0.681	0.364	0.0367	0.0382	0.0605

TABLE 8 (Continued)

		Conductors				*DC Resistance at 75°C (167°F)*		
		Stranding		*Overall*		*Copper*		*Aluminum*
Size AWG/MCM	*Area Cir. Mils*	*Quantity*	*Diam. In.*	*Diam. In.*	*Area $In.^2$*	*Uncoated ohm/ MFT*	*Coated ohm/ MFT*	*ohm/ MFT*
400	—	37	0.104	0.728	0.416	0.0321	0.0331	0.0529
500	—	37	0.116	0.813	0.519	0.0258	0.0265	0.0424
600	—	61	0.099	0.893	0.626	0.0214	0.0223	0.0353
700	—	61	0.107	0.964	0.730	0.0184	0.0189	0.0303
750	—	61	0.111	0.998	0.782	0.0171	0.0176	0.0282
800	—	61	0.114	1.03	0.834	0.0161	0.0166	0.0265

900	—	61	0.122	1.09	0.940	0.0143	0.0147	0.0235
1000	—	61	0.128	1.15	1.04	0.0129	0.0132	0.0212
1250	—	91	0.117	1.29	1.30	0.0103	0.0106	0.0169
1500	—	91	0.128	1.41	1.57	0.00858	0.00883	0.0141
1750	—	127	0.117	1.52	1.83	0.00735	0.00756	0.0121
2000	—	127	0.126	1.63	2.09	0.00643	0.00662	0.0106

These resistance values are valid ONLY for the parameters as given. Using conductors having coated strands, different stranding type, and especially, other temperatures, change the resistance.

Formula for temperature change: $R_2 = R_1 [1 + \alpha(T_2 - 75)]$ where: $\alpha_{cu} = 0.00393$, $\alpha_{AL} = 0.00330$.

Class B stranding is listed as well as solid for some sizes. Its overall diameter and area is that of its circumscribing circle. The construction information is per NEMA WC8-1976 (Rev 5-1980). The resistance is calculated per National Bureau of Standards Handbook 100, dated 1966, and Handbook 109, dated 1972.

Conductors with compact and compressed stranding have about 9 percent and 3 percent, respectively, smaller bare conductor diameters than those shown. See Table 5A for actual compact cable dimensions.

The IACS conductivities used: bare copper = 100%, aluminum = 61%.

TABLE 9 AC Resistance and Reactance 600 V Cables, 3 Phase, 60 Hz, 75°C (167°F)—Three Single Conductors in Conduit

Size AWG, MCM	*Ohms to Neutral per 1000 feet*															Size AWG/ MCM
	X (Inductance) for All Wires		*AC Resistance for Uncoated Copper Wires*			*AC Resistance for Aluminum Wires*			*Effective Z at .85 PF for Uncoated Copper Wires*			*Effective Z at .85 PF for Aluminum Wires*			
	PVC, Al. Conduits	*Steel Conduit*	*PVC Conduit*	*Al. Conduit*	*Steel Conduit*	*PVC Conduit*	*Al. Conduit*	*Steel Conduit*	*PVC Conduit*	*Al. Conduit*	*Steel Conduit*	*PVC Conduit*	*Al. Conduit*	*Steel Conduit*	
14	.058	.073	3.1	3.1	3.1	—	—	—	2.7	2.7	2.7	—	—	—	14
12	.054	.068	2.0	2.0	2.0	3.2	3.2	3.2	1.7	1.7	1.7	2.8	2.8	2.8	12
10	.050	.063	1.2	1.2	1.2	2.0	2.0	2.0	1.1	1.1	1.1	1.8	1.8	1.8	10
8	.052	.065	0.78	0.78	0.78	1.3	1.3	1.3	0.69	0.69	0.70	1.1	1.1	1.1	8
6	.051	.064	0.49	0.49	0.49	0.81	0.81	0.81	0.44	0.45	0.45	0.71	0.72	0.72	6
4	.048	.060	0.31	0.31	0.31	0.51	0.51	0.51	0.29	0.29	0.30	0.46	0.46	0.46	4
3	.047	.059	0.25	0.25	0.25	0.40	0.41	0.40	0.23	0.24	0.24	0.37	0.37	0.37	3
2	.045	.057	0.19	0.20	0.20	0.32	0.32	0.32	0.19	0.19	0.20	0.30	0.30	0.30	2
1	.046	.057	0.15	0.16	0.16	0.25	0.26	0.25	0.16	0.16	0.16	0.24	0.24	0.25	1

1/0	.044	.055	0.12	0.13	0.12	0.20	0.21	0.20	0.13	0.13	0.13	0.19	0.20	0.20	1/0
2/0	.043	.054	0.10	0.10	0.10	0.16	0.16	0.16	0.11	0.11	0.11	0.16	0.16	0.16	2/0
3/0	.042	.052	0.077	0.082	0.079	0.13	0.13	0.13	0.088	0.092	0.094	0.13	0.13	0.14	3/0
4/0	.041	.051	0.062	0.067	0.063	0.10	0.11	0.10	0.074	0.078	0.080	0.11	0.11	0.11	4/0
250	.041	.052	0.052	0.057	0.054	0.085	0.090	0.086	0.056	0.070	0.073	0.094	0.098	0.10	250
300	.041	.051	0.044	0.049	0.045	0.071	0.076	0.072	0.059	0.063	0.065	0.082	0.086	0.088	300
350	.040	.050	0.038	0.043	0.039	0.061	0.066	0.063	0.053	0.058	0.060	0.073	0.077	0.080	350
400	.040	.049	0.033	0.038	0.035	0.054	0.059	0.055	0.049	0.053	0.056	0.066	0.071	0.073	400
500	.039	.048	0.027	0.032	0.029	0.043	0.048	0.045	0.043	0.048	0.050	0.057	0.061	0.064	500
600	.039	.048	0.023	0.028	0.025	0.036	0.041	0.038	0.040	0.044	0.047	0.051	0.055	0.058	600
750	.038	.048	0.019	0.024	0.021	0.029	0.034	0.031	0.036	0.040	0.043	0.045	0.049	0.052	750
1000	.037	.046	0.015	0.019	0.018	0.023	0.027	0.025	0.032	0.036	0.040	0.039	0.042	0.046	1000

Notes:

1. These values are based on the following constants: UL-type RHH wires with Class B stranding, in cradled configuration. Wire conductives are 100% IACS copper, and 61% IACS aluminum, and aluminum conduit is 45% IACS. Capacitive reactance is ignored since it is negligible at these voltages.

These resistance values are valid only at 75°C (167°F) and for the parameters as given, but are representative for 600-volt wire types operating at 60 Hz.

2. "Effective Z" is defined as R^x cos(theta) + X^x sin(theta), where "theta" is the power factor angle of the circuit. Multiplying current by effective impedance gives a good approximation for line to neutral voltage drop. Effective impedance values in this table are valid only at .85 power factor.

For another circuit power factor (PF), effective impedance (Ze) can be calculated from R and X values given in this table as follows:

$$Ze = R^x \, PF + X^x \sin[\arccos(PF)]$$

B. EXAMPLES

Selection of Conductors. In the following examples, the results are generally expressed in amperes. To select conductor sizes, refer to Tables 310-16 through 310-31 and the Notes that pertain to such tables.

Voltage. For uniform application of Articles 210, 215, and 220, a nominal voltage of 120, 120/240, 240, and 208Y/120 volts shall be used in computing the ampere load on the conductor.

Fractions of an Ampere. Except where the computations result in a major fraction of an ampere (0.5 or larger), such fractions may be dropped.

Ranges. For the computation of the range loads in these examples, Column A of Table 220-19 has been used. For optional methods, see Columns B and C of Table 220-19.

SI Units. For SI units: one square foot = 0.093 square meter; one foot = 0.3048 meter.

Example No. 1(a) One-Family Dwelling

The dwelling has a floor area of 1500 square feet exclusive of unoccupied cellar, unfinished attic, and open porches. Appliances are a 12-kW range and a 5.5-kW, 240-volt dryer. Assume range and dryer kW ratings equivalent to kVA ratings in accordance with Sections 220-18 and 220-19.

Computed Load [see Section 220-10(a)]

General lighting load: 1500 sq. ft. at 3 volt-amperes per sq. ft. = 4500 volt-amperes.

Minimum Number of Branch Circuits Required [see Section 220-2(b)]

General lighting load: 4500 volt-amperes ÷ 120 volts = 37.5 A. This requires three 15-A 2-wire or two 20-A 2-wire circuits.

Small appliance load: two 2-wire 20-A circuits [see Section 220-4(b)].

Laundry load: one 2-wire 20-A circuit [see Section 220-4(c)].

Minimum Size Feeder Required [see Section 220-10(a)]

General lighting	4500 VA
Small appliance load	3000 VA
Laundry	1500 VA
Total general light and small appliance	9000 VA
3000 volt-amperes at 100%	3000 VA
9000 − 3000 = 6000 volt-amperes at 35%	2100 VA
Net general lighting and small appliance load	5100 VA
Range load (see Table 220-19)	8000 VA
Dryer load (see Table 220-18)	5500 VA
Total load	18,600 VA

For 120/240-volt 3-wire single-phase service or feeder:

18,600 VA ÷ 240 V = 77.5 A

Net computed load exceeds 10 kVA. Service conductors shall be 100 amperes [see Section 230-42(b)(2)].

Neutral for feeder and service

Lighting and small appliance load	5100 VA
Range load, 8000 volt-amperes at 70%	5600 VA
Dryer load, 5500 volt-amperes at 70%	3850 VA
Total	14,550 VA

14,550 VA ÷ 240 V = 60.6 A

Example No. 1(b) One-Family Dwelling

Same conditions as Example No. 1(a), plus addition of one 6-ampere, 230-volt room air-conditioning unit and one 12-ampere, 115-volt room air-conditioning unit,* one 8-ampere, 115-volt rated disposal, and one 10-ampere, 120-volt rated dishwasher.* See Article 430 for general motors and Article 440, Part G, for air-conditioning equipment. Motors have nameplate ratings of 115 V and 230 V for use on 120-V and 240-V nominal voltage systems.

From previous Example No. 1(a), feeder current is 78 amperes (3-wire 240 volts).

	Line A	*Neutral*	*Line B*
Amperes from Example No. 1(a)	78	61	78
One 230-V air conditioner	6		6
One 115-V air conditioner and 120 V dishwasher	12	12	10
One 115-V disposal		8	8
25% of largest motor (Section 430-24)	3	3	2
Amperes per line	99	84	104

* For feeder neutral, use largest of the two appliances for unbalance.

Example No. 2(a) Optional Calculation for One-Family Dwelling Heating Larger Than Air Conditioning (See Section 220-30)

Dwelling has a floor area of 1500 square feet exclusive of unoccupied cellar, unfinished attic, and open porches. It has a 12-kW range, a 2.5-kW water heater, a 1.2-kW dishwasher, 9 kW of electric space heating installed in five rooms, a 5-kW clothes dryer, and a 6-ampere, 230-volt room air-conditioning unit. Assume range, water heater, dishwasher, space heating, and clothes dryer kW ratings equivalent to kVA.

Air conditioner kVA is 6 × 230 ÷ 1000
= 1.38 kVA

1.38 kVA is less than the connected load of 9 kVA of space heating; therefore, the air-conditioner load need not be included in the service calculation (see Section 220-21).

1500 sq. ft. at 3 volt-amperes	4.5 kVA
Two 20-amp. appliance outlet circuits at 1500 volt-amperes each	3.0 kVA
Laundry circuit	1.5 kVA
Range (at nameplate rating)	12.0 kVA
Water heater	2.5 kVA
Dishwasher	1.2 kVA
Clothes dryer	5.0 kVA
	29.7 kVA
First 10 kVA of other load at 100%	= 10.0 kVA
Remainder of other load at 40% (19.7 kVA × .4) =	7.9 kVA
Total of other load =	17.9 kVA
9 kVa of heat at 40% (9 × .4) =	3.6 kVA
Total load =	21.5 kVA

Calculated load for service size
21.5 kVA = 21,500 volt-amperes
21,500 VA ÷ 240 volts = 90 amperes

Therefore, this dwelling may be served by a 100-ampere service.

Feeder Neutral Load (per Section 220-22)

1500 sq. ft. at 3 volt-amperes	4500 VA
Three 20-amp. circuits at 1500 volt-amperes	4500 VA
Total	9000 VA
3000 volt-amperes at 100%	3000 VA
9000 VA − 3000 VA = 6000 volt-amperes at 35%	2100 VA
	5100 VA
Range—8 kVA at 70%	5600 VA
Clothes dryer—5 kVA at 70%	3500 VA
Dishwasher	1200 VA
Total	15,400 VA

15,400 VA ÷ 240 V = 64.2 A

Example No. 2(b) Optional Calculation for One-Family Dwelling Air Conditioning Larger Than Heating (See Section 220-30)

Dwelling has a floor area of 1500 square feet exclusive of unoccupied cellar, unfinished attic, and open porches. It has two 20-ampere small appliance circuits, one 20-ampere laundry circuit, two 4-kW wall-mounted ovens, one 5.1-kW counter-mounted cooking unit, a 4.5-kW water heater, a 1.2-kW dishwasher, a 5-kW combination clothes washer and dryer, six 7-ampere, 230-volt room air-conditioning units, and a 1.5-kW permanently installed bathroom space heater. Assume wall-mounted ovens, counter-mounted cooking unit, water heater, dishwasher, and combination clothes washer and dryer kW ratings equivalent to kVA.

Air Conditioning kVA Calculation

Total amperes: 6 × 7 = 42.00 A
42 × 240 ÷ 1000 = 10.08 kVA of air-conditioned load assume P.F. = 1.0.

Load Included at 100%

Air conditioning (see below)
Space heater (omit; see Section 220-21)

Other Load		kVA	
1500 sq. ft. at 3 volt-amperes		4.5	
Two 20-amp. small appliance circuits at 1500 volt-amperes		3.0	
Laundry circuit		1.5	
2 ovens		8.0	
1 cooking unit		5.1	
Water heater		4.5	
Dishwasher		1.2	
Washer/dryer		5.0	
Total other load		32.8	
1st 10 kVA at 100%		10.0	kVA
Remainder at 40% (22.8 kVA × .4)		9.12	kVA
Total other load		19.12	kVA
Other load	19.12 kVA		
Air conditioning	10.08 kVA		
	29.2 kVA	= 29,200 volt-amperes	

29,200 VA ÷ 240 V = 122 A (service rating)

Feeder Neutral Load (per Section 220-22)

(It is assumed that the two-kVA wall-mounted ovens are supplied by one branch circuit, the 5.1-kVA counter-mounted cooking unit by a separate circuit.)

1500 sq. ft. at 3 volt-amperes	4500 VA
Three 20-amp circuits at 1500 volt-amperes	4500 VA
Total	9000 VA
3000 volt-amperes at 100%	3000 VA
9000 VA − 3000 VA = 6000 volt-amperes at 35%	2100 VA
Total	5100 VA

Two 4-kVA ovens plus one 5.1-kVA cooking unit totals 13.1 kVA. Table 220-19 permits 55% demand factor.

13.1 kVA × .55 = 7.2-kVA feeder capacity

7200 VA × 70% for neutral load	5040 VA
Clothes washer/dryer − 5 kVA × 70% for neutral load	3500 VA
Dishwasher	1200 VA
Total	14,840 VA

14,840 W ÷ 240 V = 61.83, use 62 A

Example No. 3 Store Building

A store 50 feet by 60 feet, or 3000 square feet, has 30 feet of show window. There are a total of 80 duplex receptacles. The service is 120/240-volt, single-phase (3-wire service).

Computed Load (Section 220-10)

*General lighting load: 3000 sq. ft. at 3 volt-amperes per sq. ft. × 1.25	11,250 VA
Show window lighting load: 30 feet at 200 volt-amperes per foot	6000 VA
Receptacle load (Section 220-13)	
80 receptacles at 180 VA = 14,400 VA;	

10,000 VA at 100%	10,000 VA
(14,400 − 10,000) VA at 50%	2200 VA
Outside sign circuit [Section 600-6(c)]: 1200 volt-amperes	1200 VA
Total	30,650 VA

Minimum Number of Branch Circuits Required

General lighting load: 11,250 volt-amperes ÷ 240 volts = 47 amperes for 3-wire, 120/240. The lighting load may be served by 2-wire or 3-wire, 15- or 20-ampere circuits with combined capacity equal to 47 amperes or greater for 3-wire circuits or 94 amperes or greater for 2-wire circuits.

Show Window

6000 volt-amperes ÷ 240 volts = 25 amperes for 3-wire, 120/240. The show window lighting may be served by 2-wire or 3-wire circuits with a capacity equal to 25 amperes or greater for 3-wire circuits or 50 amperes or greater for 2-wire circuits.

Receptacles: Receptacles required by Section 210-62 are assumed to be included in the receptacle load above if these receptacles do not supply the show window lighting load. Receptacle load: 14,400 volt-amperes ÷ 240 volts = 60 amperes for 3-wire, 120/240. The receptacle load may be served by 2-wire or 3-wire circuits with a capacity equal to 60 amperes or greater for 3-wire circuits or 120 amperes or greater for 2-wire circuits.

Minimum Size Feeders (or Service Conductors) Required (Section 215-3)

For 120/240-volt, 3-wire system:

$$30{,}650 \text{ VA} \div 240 \text{ V} = 128 \text{ A}$$

* The above examples assume that the entire lighting load is continuous. The general lighting

load is increased 125 percent in accordance with Section 220-10(b).

In the example, 125 percent of the actual connected lighting load (8500 VA × 1.25 = 10,625 VA) is less than 125 percent of the load from Table 220-3(b), so the minimum lighting load from Table 220-3(b) is used in the calculation. Had the actual lighting load been greater than the value computed from Table 220-3(b), 125 percent of the actual connected lighting load would have been used.

Example No. 4(a) Multifamily Dwelling

Multifamily dwelling having 40 dwelling units.

Meters in two banks of 20 each and individual subfeeders to each dwelling unit.

One-half of the dwelling units are equipped with electric ranges not exceeding 12 kW each. Assume range kW rating equivalent to kVA rating in accordance with Section 220-19. Other half of ranges are gas ranges.

Area of each dwelling unit is 840 square feet.

Laundry facilities on premises available to all tenants. Add no circuit to individual dwelling unit. Add 1500 volt-amperes for each laundry circuit to house load and add to the example as a "house load."

Computed Load for Each Dwelling Unit (Article 220)

General lighting load: 840 sq. ft. at 3 volt-amperes per sq. ft.	2520 VA
Special appliance load: electric range (Section 220-19)	8000 VA

Minimum Number of Branch Circuits Required for Each Dwelling Unit (Section 220-4)

General lighting load: 2520 volt-amperes ÷ 120 volts = 21 amperes or two 15-ampere, 2-wire circuits; or two 20-ampere, 2-wire circuits.

Small appliance load: Two 2-wire circuits of No. 12 wire [see Section 220-4(b)].

Range circuit: 8000 volt-amperes ÷ 240 volts = 33 amperes or a circuit of two No. 8's and one No. 10 as permitted by Section 220-22. (See Section 210-19.)

Minimum Size Subfeeder Required for Each Dwelling Unit (Section 215-2)

Computed load (Article 220)	
General lighting load	2520 VA
Small appliance load, two 20-ampere circuits	3000 VA
Total computed load (without ranges)	5520 VA
Application of demand factor	
3000 volt-amperes at 100%	3000 VA
2520 volt-amperes at 35%	882 VA
Net computed load (without ranges)	3882 VA
Range load	8000 VA
Net computed load (with ranges)	11,882 VA

Size of Each Subfeeder (see Section 215-3)

For 120/240-volt, 3-wire system (without ranges):

Net computed load: 3882 VA ÷ 240 V = 16.2 A

For 120/240-volt, 3-wire system (with ranges):

Net computed load: 11,882 VA ÷ 240 V = 49.5 A

Subfeeder neutral:	
Lighting and small appliance load	3882 VA
Range load, 8000 volt-amperes at 70% (see Section 220-22) (not included for	5600 VA

apartments without electric range)

Net computed load (neutral)	9482 VA

9482 VA ÷ 240 V = 39.5 A

Minimum Size Feeders Required from Service Equipment to Meter Bank (for 20 Dwelling Units—10 with Ranges)

Total computed load	
Lighting and small appliance load, 20 × 5520 volt-amperes	110,400 VA
Application of demand factor	
3000 volt-amperes at 100%	3000 VA
107,400 volt-amperes at 35%	37,950 VA
Net computed lighting and small appliance load	40,590 VA
Range load, 10 ranges (less than 12 kVA, Col. A, Table 220-19)	25,000 VA
Net computed load (with ranges)	65,590 VA

For 120/240-volt, 3-wire system:

Net computed load: 65,590 VA ÷ 240 V = 273 A

Feeder neutral:	
Lighting and small appliance load	40,590 VA
Range load, 25,000 volt-amperes at 70% (see Section 220-22)	17,500 VA
Computed load (neutral)	58,090 VA

58,090 VA ÷ 240 V = 242 A

Further demand factor (Section 220-22)	
200 amperes at 100%	200 A
42 amperes at 70%	29 A
Net computed load (neutral)	229 A

Minimum Size Main Feeder (or Service Conductors) Required (Less Houseload) (for 40 Dwelling Units—20 with Ranges)

Total computed load lighting and small appliance load, 40 × 5520 volt-amperes	220,800 VA
Application of demand factor	
3000 volt-amperes at 100%	3000 VA
117,000 volt-amperes at 35%	40,950 VA
100,800 volt-amperes at 25%	25,200 VA
Net computed lighting and small appliance load	69,150 VA
Range load, 20 ranges (less than 12 kVA, Col. A, Table 220-19)	35,000 VA
Net computed load	104,150 VA

For 120/240-volt, 3-wire system:

Net computed load: 104,150 VA ÷ 240 V = 434 A

Feeder neutral:	
Lighting and small appliance load	69,150 VA
Range load, 35,000 volt-amperes at 70% (see Section 220-22)	24,500 VA
Computed load (neutral)	93,650 VA

93,650 VA ÷ 240 V = 390 A

Further demand factor (see Section 220-22):	
200 amperes at 100%	200 A
190 amperes at 70%	133 A
Net computed load (neutral)	333 A

See Tables 310-16 through 310-31, Notes 8 and 10.

Example No. 4(b) Optional Calculation for Multifamily Dwelling

Multifamily dwelling equipped with electric cooking and space heating or air conditioning and having 40 dwelling units.

Meters in two banks of 20 each plus house metering and individual subfeeders to each dwelling unit.

Each dwelling unit is equipped with an electric range of 8-kW nameplate rating, four 1.5-kW separately controlled 240-volt electric space heaters, and a 2.5-kW 240-volt electric water heater. Assume range, space heater, and water heater kW ratings equivalent to kVA.

A common laundry facility is available to all tenants [Section 210-52(e), Exception No. 1].

Area of each dwelling unit is 840 square feet.

Computed Load for Each Dwelling Unit (Article 220)

General lighting load	
840 sq. ft. of 3 volt-amperes per sq. ft.	2520 VA
Electric range	8000 VA
Electric heat, 6 kVA (or air conditioning if larger)	6000 VA
Electric water heater	2500 VA

Minimum Number of Branch Circuits Required for Each Dwelling Unit

General lighting load: 2520 volt-amperes ÷ 120 volts = 21 amperes or two 15-ampere 2-wire circuits or two 20-ampere 2-wire circuits.

Small appliance load: Two 2-wire circuits of No. 12 [see Section 220-3(b)].

Range circuit: 8000 volt-amperes × 80% ÷ 240 volts = 27 amperes on a circuit of three No. 10 AWG as permitted in Column C of Table 220-19.

Space heating: 6000 volt-amperes ÷ 240 volts = 25 amperes

No. of circuits (see Section 220-4).

Minimum Size Subfeeder Required for Each Dwelling Unit (Section 215-2)

Computed load (Article 220)	
General lighting load	2520 VA
Small appliance load, two 20-ampere circuits	3000 VA
Total computed load (without range and space heating)	5520 VA
Application of demand factor	
3000 volt-amperes at 100%	3000 VA
2520 volt-amperes at 35%	882 VA
Net computed load (without range and space heating)	3882 VA
Range load	6400 VA
Space heating, Section 220-15	6000 VA
Water heater	2500 VA
Net computed load for individual dwelling unit	18,782 VA

For 120/240-volt, 3-wire system:

Net computed load: 18,782 VA ÷ 240 V = 78 A

Subfeeder neutral (Section 220-22)	
Lighting and small appliance load	3882 VA
Range load 6400 at 70% (see Section 220-22)	4480 VA
Space and water heating (no neutral) 240 volt	0 VA
Net computed load (neutral)	8362 VA

8362 VA ÷ 240 V = 35 A

Minimum Size Feeder Required from Service Equipment to Meter Bank for 20 Dwelling Units

Total computed load:	
Lighting and small appliance load, 20 × 5520 volt-amperes	110,400 VA
Water and space heating load, 20 × 8500 volt-amperes	170,000 VA
Range load, 20 × 8000	160,000 VA
Net computed load (20 dwelling units)	440,400 VA
Net computed load using optional calculation (Table 220-32) 440,400 volt-amperes × .38	167,352 VA

167,352 VA ÷ 240 V = 697 A

Minimum Size Main Feeder Required (Less House Load) for 40 Dwelling Units

Total computed load	
Lighting and small appliance load, 40 × 5520 volt-amperes	220,800 VA
Water and space heating, 40 × 8500 volt-amperes	340,000 VA

Range load, 40 × 8000 volt-amperes	320,000 VA
Net computed load (40 dwelling units)	880,800 VA
Net computed load using optional calculation (Table 220-32) 880,800 volt-amperes × .28	246,624 VA

246,624 VA ÷ 240 V = 1028 A

Feeder Neutral Load for Feeder from Service Equipment to Meter Bank (for 20 Dwelling Units)

Lighting and small appliance load, 20 × 5520 volt-amperes	110,400 VA
First 3000 volt-amperes at 100%	3000 VA
107,400 volt-amperes at 35%	37,500 VA
Subtotal	40,500 VA
20 ranges = 35,000 volt-amperes at 70% (see Table 220-19 and Section 220-22)	24,500 VA
Total	65,000 VA

65,000 VA ÷ 240 V = 271 A

Further demand factor (Section 220-22)	
First 200 amperes at 100%	200 A
Balance: 71 amperes at 70%	50 A
Total	250 A

Feeder Neutral Load of Mains Feeder (Less House Load) for 40 Dwelling Units

Lighting and small appliance load, 40 × 5520 volt-amperes	220,800 VA

First 3000 volt-amperes at 100%	3000 VA
120,000 volt-amperes − 3000 volt-amperes = 117,000 volt-amperes at 35%	40,950 VA
220,800 volt-amperes − 120,000 volt-amperes = 100,800 volt-amperes at 25%	25,200 VA
Net computed lighting and small appliance load	69,150 VA
40 Ranges = 55,000 volt-amperes at 70%	38,500 VA
(see Table 220-19 and Section 220-22)	
Total	107,650 VA

107,650 VA ÷ 240 V = 449 A

Further demand factor (Section 220-22)	
First 200 amperes at 100%	200 A
Balance: 249 amperes at 70%	174 A
Total	374 A

Example No. 5(a) Multifamily Dwelling Served at 208Y/120 Volts, Three Phase

All conditions and calculations the same as for Multifamily Dwelling [Example No. 4(a)] served at 120/240 volts, single phase except as follows: service to each dwelling unit shall be two-phase legs and neutral.

Minimum Number of Branch Circuits Required for Each Dwelling Unit (Section 220-4)

Range circuit: 8000 volt-amperes ÷ 208 volts = 38 amperes or a circuit of two No. 8 and one No. 10 as permitted by Section 220-22.

Minimum Size Subfeeder Required for Each Dwelling Unit (Section 215-2)

For 120/208-volt, 3-wire system (without ranges):

Net computed load: 3882 VA ÷ 208 V = 18.7 A

For 120/208-volt, 3-wire system (with ranges):

Net computed load: 11,882 VA ÷ 208 V = 57.1 A

Subfeeder neutral: 9482 VA ÷ 208 V = 45.6 A

Minimum Size Feeders Required from Service Equipment to Meter Bank (for 20 Dwelling Units—10 with Ranges)

For 208Y/120-volt, 3-phase, 4-wire system:

Ranges: maximum number between any two phase legs = 4. Twice 4 = 8. Table 220-19 Demand = 23,000 volt-amperes.

Per phase demand: 23,000 volt-amperes ÷ 2 = 11,500 volt-amperes.

Equivalent 3-phase load = 34,500 volt-amperes.

Net computed load (total): 40,590 volt-amperes + 34,500 volt-amperes = 75,090 volt-amperes.

75,090 VA ÷ (208)(1.732) = 208.4 A

Feeder neutral size:

40,590 VA + 34,500 VA at 70% = 64,700 VA

Net computed neutral load:

64,700 VA ÷ (208)(1.732) = 179.6 A

Minimum Size Main Feeder (Less House Load) (for 40 Dwelling Units—20 with Ranges)

For 208Y/120-volt, 3-phase, 4-wire system:

Ranges: maximum number between any two phase legs = 7. Twice 7 = 14. Table 220-19 Demand = 29,000 volt-amperes.

Per phase demand: 29,000 ÷ 2 = 14,500 volt-amperes.

Equivalent 3-phase load: 43,500 volt-amperes.

Net computed load (total): 69,150 volt-amperes + 43,500 volt-amperes = 112,650 volt-amperes

112,650 VA ÷ (208)(1.732) = 312.7 A

Main feeder neutral size:

69,150 VA + 43,500 VA at 70% = 99,600 VA

99,600 volt-amperes
÷ (208)(1.732) = 276.5 amperes

Further demand factor (Section 220-22)	
200 amperes at 100%	200.0 A
76.5 amperes at 70%	53.6 A
Net computed load	253.6 A

Example No. 5(b) Optional Calculation for Multifamily Dwelling Served at 208Y/120 Volts, Three Phase

All conditions and calculations the same as for Optional Calculations for Multifamily Dwelling [Example No. 4(b)] served at 120/240 volt, single phase except as follows:

Service to each dwelling unit shall be two-phase legs and neutral.

Minimum Number of Branch Circuits Required for Each Dwelling Unit (Section 220-4)

Range circuit: 8000 volt-amperes at 80% ÷ (208) = 30.7 amperes or a circuit of two No. 8's and one No. 10 as permitted by Section 220-22.

Space heating: 6000 volt-amperes ÷ 208 volts = 28.8 amperes. Two 20-ampere, 2-pole circuits required, No. 12.

Minimum Size Subfeeder Required for Each Dwelling Unit

Computed load (120/208-volt, 3-wire circuit):

Net computed load: 18,782 volt-amperes ÷ 208 volts = 90.3 amperes.

Net computed load (neutral) [(3882 volt-amperes ÷ 2) ÷ (120 volts)] + [(6400 volt-amperes × .07) ÷ (208 volts)] = 37.7 amperes.

Minimum Size Feeder Required for Service Equipment to Meter Bank (20 Dwelling Units)

Net computed load: 167,352 volt-amperes ÷ (208)(1.732) = 464.9 amperes.

Feeder neutral load:

65,090 VA ÷ (208)(1.732) = 180.67 A

Minimum Size Main Feeder Required (Less House Load) (40 Dwelling Units)

Net computed load: 246,624 volt-amperes ÷ (208)(1.732) = 685.1 amperes

Main feeder neutral load:

107,650 volt-amperes
÷ (208)(1.732) = 298.8 amperes

Further demand factor	
(Section 220-22)	
200 amperes at 100%	200.0 A
98.8 amperes at 70%	69.2 A
Net computed load	269.2 A

Example No. 6 Maximum Demand for Range Loads

Table 220-19, Column A, applies to ranges not over 12 kW. The application of Note 1 to ranges over 12 kW (and not over 27 kW) is illustrated in the following examples:

A. Ranges All the Same Rating

Assume 24 ranges each rated 16 kW. From Column A the maximum demand for 24 ranges of 12 kW rating is 39 kW.

16 kW exceeds 12 kW by 4.
5% × 4 = 20% (5% increase for each kW in excess of 12).
39 kW × 20% = 7.8 kW increase.
39 + 7.8 = 46.8 kW: value to be used in selection of feeders.

B. Ranges of Unequal Rating

Assume:

5 ranges each rated 11 kW
2 ranges each rated 12 kW
20 ranges each rated 13.5 kW
3 ranges each rated 18 kW

5 × 12 =	60	Use 12 kW for range rated less than 12
2 × 12 =	24	
20 × 13.5 =	270	
3 × 18 =	54	
30	408 kW	

408 ÷ 30 = 13.6 kW (average to be used for computation)

From Column A the demand for 30 ranges of 12 kW rating is 15 + 30 = 45 kW.

13.6 exceeds 12 by 1.6 (use 2).
5% × 2 = 10% (5% increase for each kW in excess of 12).
45 kW × 10% = 4.5 kW increase.
45 + 4.5 = 49.5 kW = value to be used in selection of feeders.

Example No. 8 Motors, Conductors, Overload, and Short-Circuit and Ground-Fault Protection

(See Sections 430-6, 430-7, 430-22, 430-24, 430-32, 430-34, 430-52, 430-62, and Tables 430-150 and 430-152.)

Determine the conductor size, the motor overload protection, the branch-circuit short-circuit and ground-fault protection, and the feeder protection, for one 25-horsepower squirrel-cage induction motor (full-voltage starting, service factor 1.15, Code letter F), and two 30-horsepower wound-rotor induction motors (40°C rise), on a 460-volt, 3-phase, 60-Hertz supply.

Conductor Loads

The full-load current of the 25-horsepower motor is 34 amperes (Table 430-150). A full-load current of 34 amperes × 1.25 = 42.5 amperes (Section 430-22). The full-load current of the 30-horsepower motor is 40 amperes (Table 430-150). A full-load current of 40 amperes × 1.25 = 50 amperes (Section 430-22).

The feeder ampacity will be 125 percent of 40 plus 40 plus 34, or 124 amperes (Section 430-24).

Overload and Short-Circuit and Ground-Fault Protection

Overload. Where protected by a separate overload device, the 25-horsepower motor, with full-load current of 34 amperes, must have overload protection of not over 42.5 amperes [Sections 430-6(a) and 430-32(a)(1)]. Where protected by a separate overload device, the 30-horsepower motor, with full-load current of 40 amperes, must have overload protection of not over 50 amperes [Sections 430-6(a) and 430-32(a)(1)]. If the overload protection is not sufficient to start the motor or to carry the load, it may be increased according to Section 430-34. For a motor marked "thermally protected," overload protection is provided by the thermal protector [see Sections 430-7(a)(12) and 430-32(a)(2)].

Branch-Circuit Short-Circuit and Ground-Fault. The branch circuit of the 25-horsepower motor must have branch-circuit short-circuit and ground-fault protection of not over 300 percent for a nontime-delay fuse (Table 430-152) or $3.00 \times 34 = 102$ amperes. The next smaller standard size fuse is 100 amperes. The fuse size may be increased to 110 or 125 amperes (Section 430-52, Exception No. 1) if the 100-ampere fuse is not sufficient for the starting current of the motor.

For the 30-horsepower motor, the branch-circuit short-circuit and ground-fault protection is 150 percent (Table 430-152) or $1.50 \times 40 = 60$ amperes. Where the maximum value of branch-circuit short-circuit and ground-fault protection is not sufficient to start the motor, the value for a nontime-delay fuse may be increased to 400 percent [Section 430-52, Exception No. 2(a)].

Feeder Circuit. The maximum rating of the feeder short-circuit and ground-fault protection device is based on the sum of the largest branch-circuit protective device (110-ampere fuse) plus the sum of the full-load currents of the other motors or 110 plus 40 plus 40 = 190 amperes. The nearest standard fuse which does not exceed this value is 175 amperes [Section 430-62(a)].

418

1-800-

458-5400